A COMPARATIVE STUDY OF CROWD BEHAVIOUR AT TWO MAJOR MUSIC EVENTS

Chris Kemp, Iain Hill, Mick Upton

This report was commissioned by the Buckinghamshire Chilterns University College following concerns expressed about the safety of live events by practitioners and public alike. The report was supported by the UKCMA, Showsec, Show and Event Security, Metropolis and Gaming international Ltd who gave their full co-operation with the writing of the Report and supported both the managers and researchers during the process. Students from the Centre for Crowd Management Studies were tasked to collect the data and this was processed through SNAP. The data was triangulated through utilising participant observation, questionnaires, gate calculations and fill capacities to give as comprehensive and valuable data as possible.

Entertainment Technology Press

A COMPARATIVE STUDY OF CROWD BEHAVIOUR AT TWO MAJOR MUSIC EVENTS

© Chris Kemp, Iain Hill, Mick Upton

First edition Published July 2004 by
Entertainment Technology Press Ltd
The Studio, High Green, Great Shelford, Cambridge CB2 5EG
Internet: www.etnow.com

ISBN 1 904031 25 0

A title within the
Entertainment Technology Press Safety Series
Series editor: John Offord
in association with Buckinghamshire New University

CODE / CB001

A COMPARATIVE STUDY OF CROWD BEHAVIOUR AT TWO MAJOR MUSIC EVENTS

Chris Kemp
Iain Hill
Mick Upton

ENTERTAINMENT
TECHNOLOGY PRESS

Safety Series

CONTENTS

I CONTRIBUTORS 7

I INTRODUCTION 9
1.1   Scenario I: Eminem at the National Bowl 10
1.2   Scenario 2: Robbie Williams at Knebworth 10

2 AIMS AND OBJECTIVES OF THE REPORT 11

3 METHODOLOGY 13
3.1   Introduction 13
3.2   Data Collection and the Questionnaires 13
3.3   The Fill Capacity Methodology 14
3.4   Flow Capacities 15

4 SAMPLE 17

5 CONCERT COMMAND AND CONTROL SYSTEMS 19
5.1   Strategic Level 19
5.2   Crowd Safety Planning 20
5.3   Published Guidance 20
5.4   Space 20
5.5   Flow 22
5.6   Ingress 22
5.7   Egress 22
5.8   Tactical level 24
5.9   Control room facilities 25
5.10   The role of the ELT (Emergency Liaison Team) 25
5.11   Operational level 26

6 FINDINGS 27
6.1   Crowd Management strategies and their effect on fill
       capacities at concerts 27

6.2   The Dynamics of Ingress Flow at Live Events 29

6.2.1   Day One 29

6.2.2   Day Two 30

6.2.3   Day Three 31

6.3   The Measurement of Crowd Flow at Ingress: Cumulative
Audience Totals 31

6.4   Crowd Behaviour and Perceptions at the Eminem and Robbie
Williams Events 39

6.4.2   Crowd Behaviour and Perceptions before entering the event
arena 39

6.4.2.2   Analysis 42

6.4.3   Crowd Behaviour and Perceptions when first entering the
arena 45

6.4.3.2   Analysis 46

6.4.4   Crowd Behaviour and Perceptions at the Barrier 49

6.4.4.1   Findings 50

6.4.4.2   Analysis 50

6.4.5   Conclusions from this section of the Research 52

6.4.5.1   Conclusions from this section of the Research 53

**7   A CRITIQUE OF ESTABLISHING CROWD
CAPACITY AND DENSITY AT AN OUTDOOR
CONCERT EVENT ATTRACTING A MASS
CROWD** (produced by Mick Upton) 55

7.1   Crowd Safety at Mass Crowd Concerts 55

7.2   Current Practice 56

7.3   Pressure Loads 57

7.4   Area Design 58

7.5   Conclusions 59

            Appendix 60

**8   PRELIMINARY CONCLUSIONS TO THE
REPORT** 63

            References 67

            Publishers 68

CONTRIBUTORS

Authors

Professor Chris Kemp   Dean of Faculty of Leisure and Tourism
                              Buckinghamshire Chilterns University
                              College

Iain Hill   Artist Manager and Lecturer

Mick Upton   Crowd Management Specialist

Data Analysts
Gemma Morris
Nadine Barr

Project Managers
Katriona Baird
Annabel Harrison
Holly Marshall

Data Collection
Kim Blake
Lindsey Craft
Sarah-Marie Capaldi
Sarah Hayden
Vicky Illsley
Fikriye Karababa
Cynthia Kunsche
Chris Manning
Andrew Marsh
Christopher Manning
Sharon McConaghey
Izabella Milewska
Rose Webb

1 INTRODUCTION

With live entertainment experiencing a healthy growth belying the problems seemingly experienced in other sectors of the entertainment industry, it appears that the consumer is well serviced and satisfied in this area. Yet worldwide in 2003, 193[1] of those seemingly satisfied consumers have died whilst attending events that were legally licensed and held on established premises. The wide range of articles, papers and reports into such incidents causing fatalities identify the behaviour of the crowd and the way in which behaviour is managed as a fundamental factor, which needs to be addressed in any move to make events safer.

If the palpable improvements in Health and Safety legislation and the increased legislative control through the licensing procedure have made the concert place a safer (and more comfortable) environment, the issues that surround the management of crowd behaviour give rise to wide ranging questions that continue to divide the industry. The premise underpinning this report is based on a dearth of knowledge and understanding of crowd dynamics and patterns of crowd behaviour in the concert environment. Only through an increased understanding of crowd behaviour can the models and the systems currently utilised in crowd management be improved or modified to enable a decrease in and hopefully the eradication of, such fatalities.

The resources available to those compiling the research which contributes to this report were by no means affluent, and the report does not claim to identify definitive answers but proffers possible solutions and identifies potential areas which could lead to further research or work to modify present management strategies instituted in the live music environment. The limited scope and the necessary concentration on selective areas of crowd behaviour denote that the report seeks primarily to identify areas of tension and not to solve the problems highlighted in the data collection process. Thus the primary objective of the report is to identify a body of useable knowledge pertaining to crowd

---

1. 2003 was an exceptionally bad year for deaths at music events. The figure of 193 is the sum total of deaths at concerts in 2003 including (correct at the time of writing) those at The Station Nightclub, Rhode Island, a nightclub in Chicago where a crush developed at the foot of a set of stairs where a door had been padlocked, and at a train station in Belarus where people were leaving a concert.

behaviour that contributes to improvements in crowd safety at live music events through the refining of crowd management procedures. In the future, with feedback from the industry (and with increased resources), the methodologies and the scope of this report can be refined and improved.

This ambition cannot be achieved without the cooperation of the industry itself. The authors of the report were overwhelmed by the interest, enthusiasm and support that they received at every level from everyone involved in the management of the two concerts where the research took place. There was a feeling – especially from those who were most directly involved in the crowd management process – that this was a useful and necessary initiative. We can only hope that this first step justifies the assistance and the encouragement that we received from those in the live music industry.

1.1　Scenario 1:
Eminem at the National Bowl 21st/22nd/23rd June 2003

The National Bowl in Milton Keynes is a purpose-built venue for concerts and other events. The venue comprises a man-made bowl holding circa 65,000 spectators. The National Bowl has a free-standing stage as a permanent fixture, with gates, fences and utilities (water and electricity) in situ. The venue is easily accessible by both road and rail with excellent communication systems and car parking facilities. All access and egress to the site is lit at night and the site is easily accessible by contractor vehicles.

1.2　Scenario 2:
Robbie Williams at Knebworth 1st /2nd/3rd August 2003

This venue, in the grounds of Knebworth House, is a green-field site that has to be prepared from scratch. The licence granted for this event allowed a capacity of 125,000 spectators on each of the three nights. The road access to the venue is good, although there has always been a tendency at previous events for a bottleneck to develop once the traffic has left the A1M at Junction 8 to join the A602 and then the B656 to access the parking facilities. These facilities are fully capable of housing the volume of cars expected for an event of this size. Access by rail is not so easy; the nearest station is Knebworth Town and the larger station at Stevenage is a long distance from the venue. Contractor and emergency access to the venue is easily accessed through Old Knebworth and from Junction 6 of the A1M, which is not used by the public.

2 AIMS AND OBJECTIVES OF THE REPORT

The way in which crowds behave at live events has been the focus of much live music research as this is one of the factors directly related to event management and strategy. Firstly, access to and egress from events is a major cause of internal and external customer problems. Secondly, the behaviour of audiences and crowd managers alike, before, during and after an event is a significant factor in the enjoyment of the event by the external customer. The control exhibited by the internal customer and thus the way in which the crowd behaves, is a crucial factor in the preparation, planning and execution of strategies for events. Thus, the intelligence gathered before, during and after the event is crucial to be able to modify strategies in a changing environment. One of the main objectives of this report was to understand more about the nature of crowd behaviour and crowd management at live events and how information from this integration and interface can be applied in the concert environment.

The main aims in carrying out this research were as follows:

- to understand more about the nature of crowd behaviour and crowd management at live events and how information from the integration and interface of the audience and those managing the safety of the event can be applied in the concert environment.

- to ascertain how crowd management strategies affect fill-capacities at concerts.

- to ascertain information on the dynamics of ingress flow at live events.

- to explore the command and control systems used by the managers of the concert.

- to explore social and cultural behaviour at live music events.

- to ascertain the public's perceptions of safety and welfare.

- to explore and comment on traffic problems during the concerts.

- to identify a body of useable knowledge pertaining to crowd behaviour that contributes to improvements in crowd safety at live music events through the refining of crowd management procedures.

3 METHODOLOGY

3.1 Introduction

This research is both qualitative and quantitative in nature, seeking to integrate and deliver mutually supportive evidence to validate the findings of the report. The initial quantitative studies support the qualitative data and input from those involved in the events, video evidence, interviews and participant observation. Triangulation of the data in this way increases the validity of the findings.

3.2 Data Collection and the Questionnaires

The data collection was carried out by utilising a number of methods. Firstly, three different questionnaires were administered to the audience on each of the six days of the two concerts, culminating in 1800 responses. The questionnaires were administered in a random fashion in three areas of the concert. Firstly outside the gate whilst the audience was queuing, secondly inside the concert at random points, and thirdly at the barrier after the support artists had performed. From these three questionnaires it was hoped that responses concerning the well-being of the audience and their perceptions about health and safety at the two shows would be collected. As the questionnaire was administered, there were few spoiled responses as those administering the questionnaires were well briefed on how to ensure valid answers were obtained.

The issues explored in questionnaire one were:

- Where the respondent was going to watch the concert from
- Where the respondent intended to go once through the gate
- The perceptions of the safety and comfort of the queue
- The communication of information to the crowd
- Traffic instructions and their clarity
- How the respondent reached the venue
- How long the respondent had been queuing
- What protective clothing had they brought
- If they brought protective clothing, where did they get the information to do this?

The issues explored in questionnaire two were:

- Where the first place was that they went to when getting into the arena?
- How safe they felt in the arena and why?
- What safety problems had they observed, if any?
- Are there services that should be provided which were not?
- Where were they going to watch the main band from?
- Had they brought the right clothing for the day?
- Would they have liked information on what to wear for the day?
- How do they rate the facilities at the venue?

The issues explored in questionnaire three were:

- The perception of the audience at the front of the barrier
- How important is it to be at the front of a concert audience
- Perceptions of regulations to prohibit antisocial behaviour and audience reaction to them
- Injuries in front of stage area and their affect on the audience
- How safety features would enhance an audience's enjoyment of the concert

3.3   The Fill Capacity Methodology

The fill capacity methodology was carried out as follows:

Two parallel lines were measured from the front of stage barrier outward towards the second barrier in the two-barrier system. Metre markers were painted on the ground along these parallel lines up to a distance of 18 metres. At Knebworth, the distance between the first and second barriers was almost double that of Milton Keynes. Therefore, the measurement of 18 metres was used at both venues to ensure comparability. A researcher was placed behind the front of stage barrier at the origin of each parallel line. A second researcher was placed in the pit area in front of the first barrier in a position where a set of lines could be viewed at all times. Each researcher behind the barrier had a zeroed stopwatch and timing commenced as the gates opened. Each time a metre line was filled by the crowd on each of the parallel lines, to the left and right of stage, the second researcher would signal for the time taken to reach that metre line to be recorded. This process was carried out until all 18-metre markers were covered on both parallel lines.

3.4 Flow Capacities

The flow capacities were calculated in different ways at the two concerts, as it became clear that there were two very different scenarios at Knebworth and Milton Keynes. At the National Bowl, the focus of the study was on the fluidity of people accessing through gates 3 and 6 and thus the following system was utilised:

Researchers were placed in front of the gate lanes well before opening and a timer was also utilised so that all researchers would know the time which had expired during the counting period. All researchers were furnished with people counters. The flow through the gates was calculated at one-minute intervals for the first 30 minutes after the gates had been opened. The timer shouted the minute periods and the researchers noted down the number on the people counters. The total was cumulative as to reset the counters would have meant that researchers may have missed audience members.

At Knebworth, the focus was more on the number of people congregating in the arena at any one time and how extraneous elements such as traffic congestion, parking, and the sheer volume of people attending the concert, affected access and egress. The research was carried out by placing people counters on the gates for the first 15 minutes of every hour and then calculating the flow-capacity per hour for each of the lanes that were monitored. At the same time, a separate group of students would establish how many of the lanes were operational at each of the gates at that particular time. Using a spreadsheet developed for this purpose, entering the data every hour allowed for the calculation of a cumulative capacity figure at any one time.

Participant observation and general observation of similarities and differences between the two concerts researched was carried out at all times and a large amount of this qualitative evidence was collected to support the quantitative data. Video evidence of crowd movement, fill-capacity, and flow-capacity was also recorded at each day of the two events. This was also analysed and integrated into the findings.

4 SAMPLE

The hand-administered questionnaires were targeted at those respondents outside the gates, inside the arena, and at the barrier.

In total, the sample of completed questionnaires represented the views of 1800 concert attendees. Analysis of the questionnaire population shows an even spread across geographic areas, i.e. no significant regional bias. Similarly, there is a balanced split between male and female respondents in all three questionnaire categories over the six concert days. Correspondingly, a balance was maintained between differing age groups, so that a wide range of responses was taken demographically.

It is difficult to identify a sample typology for the other two areas of experimentation (fill- and flow-capacities), as they comprised random audience samples, which could not be regulated.

5 CONCERT COMMAND AND CONTROL SYSTEMS

Show and Event Security Ltd. undertook the planning and subsequent management of crowd safety at the six concerts studied. This research considered the level of ability that a crowd management company had to implement the concept of command and control for each event. A Command and Control concept is considered to operate on three levels: Strategic, Tactical, and Operational.

5.1 Strategic Level

This is defined as the ability to prepare documentation necessary for a crowd safety management operation and secure necessary resources. To include:

- Health and Safety at Work Policy
- Event Risk Analysis
- Risk Assessment
- Risk Reduction/Management
- Safety Management Plan
- Securing necessary resources
- Securing necessary equipment/clothing/transport
- Designing contingency action plans
- Insurance
- Staff Welfare

At a strategic level it was identified that comprehensive documentation had been prepared, submitted to, and approved by, local authorities for all six concert days studied. Documents included all of those elements outlined above. The welfare of the security staff was a prime concern in terms of catering, high profile uniform, protective clothing, earplugs, sun block, radio equipment, and site vehicles. The promoter at each concert provided public welfare services. A medical team led by a chief medical officer supported by the ambulance service and an experienced welfare services team that dealt with issues ranging from lost children to alcohol abuse, were all present.

5.2 Crowd Safety Planning

Of particular interest to this research was the fact that crowd safety management is not recognised as a social science and consequently no training courses are currently available to offer a nationally recognised qualification indicating the level of competence of the appointed crowd manager. A lack of a formal qualification dictates that operational planning for concert crowd safety is largely a generic exercise that is dependent on the planner's previous experience. However, help is available in the form of published guidance.

5.3 Published Guidance

Guidance for concert planning is published in the form of *The Event Safety Guide (2001),* published by the Health and Safety Executive and popularly referred to as the 'Purple Guide', a reference to the distinctive colour of its cover. In order to form a balanced opinion of crowd management planning at the concerts that were studied, it was necessary to review the crowd management chapter of the Purple Guide with regard to advice offered on the key issues of calculating space (density) and pedestrian systems (crowd flow). The information gained from this literature review was then used as an aid to evaluate the actual crowd management plan that had been prepared. Having reviewed the prepared plan, it was evaluated by an observational study.

5.4 Space

Page 15, paragraph 87, and page 22, paragraph 122, of The Purple Guide, recommend that the occupant capacity for a concert event should be established on the basis of 0.5m² (two persons per square metre) for space with a clear view of the stage. Capacity is subject to the approval of the local fire officer who would need to be satisfied that an emergency evacuation exit capability is available. In view of the important role played by the fire officer in approving systems' design, a further review was undertaken in the *Guide to Fire Precautions in Existing Places of Entertainment and Like Premises (a),* popularly referred to as the Yellow or Primrose guide. Page 43 paragraph 5.20 of the Yellow guide, under the title 'Occupant load factors', confirmed that 0.5m² was the recommended criterion for establishing crowd density at a pop concert and like occasion. A review of the event plans confirmed that capacity and anticipated density level at the three National Bowl concerts for 65,000 people each, and for three concerts at Knebworth with an attendance of 125,000, each concert had been based on guidance recommendation of 0.5m².

The simple calculation recommended by published guidance is, however, open to question as it appears to overlook the issue of how a crowd will interpret and use the space that has been provided, particularly during a prolonged stay in extreme weather conditions. At five of the six concerts studied, the weather was very hot and it was found that in such conditions a great many people felt the need to sit down. At the National Bowl, crowd use of space was not a problem as the venue is designed in amphitheatre style and those who wished to sit simply moved to the grass slopes at the back and sides. The problem was more noticeable at Knebworth, which is a fenced flat green field. A great many people simply sat down where they were, which meant they occupied double the amount of space allowed for them.

People sitting down at the Knebworth concerts caused three problems: firstly, crowd migration necessary to purchase food and drink or use facilities, was very difficult. Secondly, the mass bulk of the crowd stood up when Robbie Williams came on stage, eliciting a dynamic crowd surge at the rear of the crowd caused by people attempting to occupy newly available space. It must be said, however, that this surge was of a short duration and no crushing incidents were observed at the three concerts that were studied at Knebworth. Thirdly, large numbers of the audience did not have direct sight of the stage and others could see neither stage nor screen. Other audience members were reliant on the screens for any view of the performance at all.

This situation led to crowds emerging anywhere that a screen was visible and as such, these groups had no direct reference to the main audience. In particular, a stream of attendees tailed back through the trees that lined the concessions area to the stage right, blocking the normal flow of the bulk of the audience to the concession stands and to the water and toilet facilities. Whilst this did not in itself cause any particular danger, it did lead to an increase in the sense of frustration that many people expressed regarding the difficulty of migration across the site. For others, the failure to get any direct view of the stage at all was also a major factor in contributing to a feeling amongst a large proportion of those at the fringes of the crowd, that there were too many people in the arena and that their enjoyment/comfort/safety had been compromised as a result. Dissatisfaction with the event and management was the result.

5.5 Flow

The Purple Guide offers only general advice on the design of pedestrian flow systems. For specific examples of calculations the reader is advised to consult either the Yellow Guide or the *Guide to Safety at Sports Grounds* (Green Guide) for advice on the design of pedestrian flow systems. It was therefore necessary to conduct a further review of both these guides in order to establish whether they both offered the same formula for calculating crowd flow.

5.6 Ingress

The Yellow Guide (b) advises that the amount of space required for people to move in single file is termed a *unit width*. A unit width is set by the Yellow Guide at 525mm, and a unit width is estimated to be capable of passing a flow of forty (40) persons per minute. As the Green Guide is primarily aimed at architecturally designed sports grounds with turnstile facilities, it was considered not to be relevant to this research. At both the National Bowl and Knebworth entry lanes at each gate were constructed at two-unit widths to allow for persons carrying bulky items. The plan estimate for flow was deliberately reduced by 50% from 40 to 20 persons per minute at both venues to allow for a reduced pedestrian speed due to the fact that each person was required to pass through three stages on entry: ticket check, search and ticket take. Student observation found that entry lanes easily achieved, and maintained, a flow rate of twenty (20) persons per minute.

5.7 Egress

Surprisingly, there is no recommended period for an emergency evacuation for a major outdoor concert. The question of emergency evacuation time is a matter of negotiation between the local fire officer and the crowd manager. At the two venues that were studied, both parties agreed an evacuation time of fifteen (15) minutes. The crowd management plan based its calculations for exit requirement for both venues on a unit width of 550mm with a flow rate of forty (40) persons per minute per unit width with a fifteen (15) minute evacuation time. The calculation applied for a standard 5-metre exit gate was therefore:

5000mm x 40 (persons per min) x 15 (evacuation time) = 5454 persons in 15 mins 550 (unit width).

It is interesting to compare the advice offered by the Fire Service on pedestrian flow with that offered by the Green Guide for sports grounds. Page 80, under the heading 'Recommended rates of passage' paragraph (b), advises that exit flow can be calculated at a rate of 109 persons per metre width (2 units) per minute. This formula is clearly at odds with the Yellow Guide estimate of 80 persons for 2 unit widths. Following the Green Guide formula, a flow rate of 109 persons per metre through a standard 5-metre exit gate with an evacuation time of fifteen minutes could be calculated to allow a flow volume of:

$$109 \text{ (persons per metre)} \times 5 \text{ (metres)} \times 15 \text{ (minutes)} = 8175 \text{ persons}$$

With a difference of 2721 persons for the flow rate of a single 5 metre exit gate indicated by comparing the two published guides, confusion exists with regard to the calculation of exit requirement. At the two venues that were studied, the Yellow Guide unit width flow calculation of forty (40) persons system was adopted and approved by the local authority.

An observational study of egress at both venues identified several problems, as follows. There was not enough room at either venue to construct the total exit width required for a mass crowd due to the amount of space required for ingress gates. The solution used to overcome this problem at both venues was to progressively convert ingress gates to exit gates as the arena filled up. As there was no facility to conduct ongoing calculations to determine the level of people inside the arena, conversion was based on management observation and traffic reports from the police. Unfortunately, it was noted at the first Knebworth concert that a police traffic report was inaccurate. The report given to the event control room stated that the roads were clear of traffic when in actual fact there was a major traffic jam immediately outside the venue on the A1 motorway caused by people trying to get into the venue. According to media reports later, this traffic jam proved to be so serious that many people actually missed the concert.

At the first Eminem concert at the National Bowl there was a problem at gate 3 when pedestrian flow came to a stop at one point. A crowd diversion was attempted but unfortunately radio communications failed at this point. Prompt action by a security response team quickly established that an illegal poster seller had set up shop in the middle of the gate. Once he was removed, normal flow rate was quickly established. This incident clearly demonstrated that even the actions of one person can bring egress to a complete stop, causing a high crowd density build-up.

Observation of egress at the National Bowl identified support for Smith (1991) who argued that *"flow volume has an optimum density. If this density is surpassed the obtainable rate decreases. One reason for this is that as the density increases, so does the swaying, shuffling motion of the body, as it becomes difficult to take normal sized strides, thus reducing the flow rate".*

From the analysis it was established that peak flow was only possible during the initial stage of egress. Once the density level at the gate increased, pedestrian flow rate slowed considerably; in fact flow came to a brief stop several times. The increase in crowd density appeared to be due to the sheer volume of people within the egress system as a whole.

Observation of egress at Knebworth identified that the large expanse of egress width created by the conversion of fifty-five (55) ingress gates allowed a mass crowd exit. At the first concert, however, a pinch point was identified at the exit route to the car parks, which caused a high-density crowd incident in which several people received minor injuries due to falling over. This problem was resolved at subsequent concerts by a minor alteration to the exit route. This incident supported the argument put forward by Stanton and Wanless (1993) that *"the calculation sequence should be area by area and route by route to define tight spots, bends, restrictions, etc."*

A field trial was conducted during egress at the National Bowl on day one of the Eminem concerts to test the Green Guide statement that exit flow could be calculated at a rate of 109 persons per metre per minute. A 1m gate was opened at the side of Gate 3 and people were encouraged to use it. It was found that two people could only move through a 1m gap at normal walking speed with difficulty. Initial flow rate was measured at a rate of 75 persons in the first minute; this figure was close to the Yellow Guide calculation of 80 persons for two unit widths. Flow slowed down dramatically however, as crowd density increased and at times came to a complete stop.

5.8 Tactical level

On-site management of the crowd safety plan should include:

Control room management
CCTV management
Implementation of contingency action plans
Deployment of response teams
The management of resources

At both the venues studied in this research, the concert organisers, private security, venue operator and all local authorities demonstrated a high level of commitment to public safety issues. Although the concerts at both venues were staged by the same promoter and managed by the same security company, there were marked differences between the two venues in the way that tactical management operated. These differences could be summarised as both structural and managerial. The contrasting control room facilities and the contrasting roles of the Emergency Liaison Teams (ELT) were identified as two major differences between the management and strategic development at the two events.

5.9 Control Room Facilities

At the National Bowl the crowd management operation was operated from a single portacabin that was located in the public area. The radio network was managed by a single operator without access to CCTV and no direct sight of any areas under their management. By contrast, the crowd management operation at Knebworth was run from a double stacked portacabin. The ground floor level housed a five-monitor CCTV system controlled by a single operator who also had responsibility for issuing radio equipment. At the top deck level, three radio operators with an overview of the arena controlled the network.

5.10 The Role of the ELT (Emergency Liaison Team)

The concept of an ELT came into being following a fatal crowd related accident at a concert in 1988. The Purple Guide (b) advises that *"other than at small events, it is essential that on-site accommodation is set aside as a designated emergency liaison center. While the event is running, make sure that this center is staffed continuously"*.

At both venues the police had issued a Statement of Intent which clearly indicated that they (the police) had no responsibility for public safety. The police at both venues had their own compound which housed on-site a mobile police control room and other facilities that might be needed.

It appeared that the role of the ELT was interpreted differently at the venues studied. At the National Bowl the ELT was based in the back stage area. The police operated a one monitor CCTV system at one end of the room while the local authority operated a separate single monitor portable CCTV system at the other end of the room. Each organisation controlled their own picture on screen. Separate from this, a vehicle with CCTV facilities was positioned at Gate 6 to monitor ingress and egress. The vehicle appeared to have been paid for by the local authority and monitored by the police.

The police and local authority therefore appeared to be running parallel control rooms. This was most evident at Knebworth where the ELT had an overview of the arena and was manned by a large team of officers from the emergency services. On at least one occasion it was noted that the police passed a message to the event control room to deal with people climbing on toilet roofs. In spite of the fact that the control room was at that point dealing with a potentially serious queue problem, CCTV was focused on the toilet block and a response team was diverted to deal with the climbers. This action was taken because the message came from a police officer and was therefore considered to be important.

5.11 Operational level

Minute-by-minute supervision of the crowd management plan, should include:

- Customer care and the ability to deal with complaints
- Staff supervision and welfare
- The monitoring of pedestrian flow systems
- The monitoring of crowd density levels
- The provision of accurate situational reports to control

At an operational level, all six concerts were well managed. Staff were in possession of site maps and were able to provided information to ticket holders on a range of services and facilities that were available on site. Response teams operated overtly and covertly both inside and outside the arena at both venues. Security freely responded to questions on their perceived role and responsibility.

6 FINDINGS

6.1 Crowd Management Strategies and their Effect on Fill Capacities at Concerts

	L1	R1	L2	R2	L3	R3	L4	R4	L5	R5
M1	2.06	6.5	2.09	3.33	2.04	2.5	4.5	5.4	2.22	3.46
M2	5.23	7.14	4.19	5.06	2.54	3.58	5.29	6.21	3.03	4
M3	5.43	9.28	7.14	6.19	3.24	4.44	6.1	6.47	5.16	4.05
M4	5.55	11.3	8.02	8.35	3.44	5.2	6.33	6.54	3.3	4.23
M5	6.54	13.52	9.03	9.54	4.15	5.49	6.45	7.05	3.37	4.5
M6	7.12	17.07	10.34	10.51	4.4	6.49	7.02	7.3	3.49	5.12
M7	8.36	19.02	10.49	11.37	4.57	7.12	7.17	7.36	4.03	5.37
M8	9.03	19.02	12.57	13.54	4.57	7.45	7.33	7.47	4.22	5.57
M9	9.58	19.02	13.5	14.25	4.58	8.27	7.53	8.1	4.4	6.14
M10	10.6	19.02	14.03	17.2	5.3	8.34	8.21	9.02	4.48	6.36
M11	10.24	19.02	14.27	17.52	5.3	8.34	8.21	9.02	5.1	6.53
M12	10.47	19.02	15.19	18.12	5.3	8.34	8.21	9.02	5.18	6.53
M13	12.18	19.02	16.24	18.39	5.3	8.34	8.21	9.02	5.31	6.53
M14	13.43	19.02	17.12	18.4	5.3	8.34	8.21	9.02	5.41	6.53
M15	13.52	19.02	17.36	20.05	5.3	8.34	8.21	9.02	5.55	6.53
M16	13.52	19.02	18.1	20.12	5.3	8.34	8.21	9.02	6	6.53
M17	13.52	19.02	18.1	20.12	5.3	8.34	8.21	9.02	6.17	6.53
M18	13.52	19.02	18.1	20.12	5.3	8.34	8.21	9.02	6.17	6.53

The above table shows the fill capacity times per metre for the front of stage pit area up to 18 metres from the barrier for the three Eminem shows and the first two days of the Knebworth shows. The third Knebworth show is not tabulated, as it is virtually the same in fill capacity timing as day one. At both venues, the right hand side of the stage fills in a shorter time than that of the left hand side of the stage. The reason for this is quite simple at the National Bowl: the right hand side of the stage is adjacent to Gate 3. If Gate 3 and Gate 6, the main entrances, are opened simultaneously, it takes three to five minutes to get from Gate 6 to the entry gate to the front of stage pen, whereas it only takes one minute to get from gate 3 to the pen. It is clear from video evidence that those attendees entering the arena at Gate 3 can immediately identify the access to the front of stage area as they pass it on entering the event. However, those entering from Gate 6 have to cover about six hundred metres before entering the gate to the front of stage area. In addition, video evidence identifies that at the lip of the bowl the gate entrance to the left of the stage is obscured by both the second barrier and the big screen towers, making easy access difficult.

At Knebworth, the main car parks are close to the right hand side of the stage and thus this area fills more quickly than the left hand side. However, the access to the left hand side of the stage is also relatively easy as evidenced by the quicker fill capacity than the National Bowl shows. At the National Bowl the difference between right and left fill is 6, 2 and 3 minutes respectively over the three days, whereas at the Knebworth event the difference between 18 metre fill capacities is less than a minute on each of the three days.

The foregoing analysis identifies that the audience at the Robbie Williams events filled the front of stage pen faster than the audience at the Eminem concerts. The build up of audience at Eminem was initially greater than the build up of the audience at the Robbie Williams concerts. From video evidence and participant observation, it was clear that significantly more attendees congregated outside the National Bowl in advance of the gates opening in comparison to the number of attendees congregating in advance of the gates opening at the Knebworth concerts. From interview, this build up outside the National Bowl was attributed to a number of factors, including ease of access to the Bowl, eagerness to get as close to the front as possible, the nature of the crowd and the genre of the artist.

More gates/lanes were used to allow the audience into the arena at the Robbie Williams concerts than at the Eminem concerts in line with the differing capacities identified for the events. Crowd crush and constrictions on the entry roads led to fewer audience members passing through the gates per minute at the National Bowl, which led to dissatisfaction with the queuing arrangements, as evidenced in the responses to questionnaire 1.

The greater entry opportunity afforded at the Robbie Williams concerts and the lack of congestion allowed a greater volume of audience to pass through the gates in a shorter period, as evidenced in section 5.7. Thus, the fill-capacity in the front of stage area at the Robbie Williams concert was achieved in a shorter space of time than the fill capacity in the front of stage area at the Eminem concert.

The distance from the arena entry point to the front of stage area is more at the Knebworth event than it is at the National Bowl. However, there are fewer restrictions between the gate and the front of stage at Knebworth. From video evidence, it is clear that the orientation within Knebworth takes place more quickly than at the National Bowl.

It was also clear from observations made of the Eminem concert access, video evidence and calculations made on through capacities to the venue, that owing to the constrictive nature of Gate 3 twice as many audience members were able to enter the arena through Gate 6 than Gate 3. From visual evidence and interviews, it is clear that the small bridge outside gate 3 constricted the crowd and caused heavy build-up at the start of the lanes, which made access difficult in the initial stages of entry to the venue. At gate 6, the audience queuing to enter the arena tended to fan out and pass though the lanes far more easily, and thus entry through this gate had fewer obstructions.

Demographically, the audience initially queuing at all three Robbie Williams shows was fairly widespread, whereas the audience at Eminem was generally white and male. On entry to the National Bowl, the audience was restricted to walking whereas the audience at Knebworth did not have such restrictions. This was another factor which enabled the audience at the Knebworth event to fill the front of stage area much faster than the audience at the National Bowl.

As the research into fill-capacities at the front of the stage did not identify any health and safety issues, comments and suggestions on health and safety are not appropriate here, but what is clear from video evidence is that the first people in the queue are there specifically to get as close to the front as possible. If some way of controlling ticket selling to specific areas were enabled, then a greater control of queuing possibilities would be available.

6.2 The Dynamics of Ingress Flow at Live Events
At Knebworth, the general observations that were recorded at the time that the gates were opened, were as follows:

6.2.1 Day One
Prior to the gates opening, the site preparation had been completed and the arena fully prepared. There was an orderly build-up of the crowd at each gate, controlled by the gate marshals and their supervisors, using loud-hailers. The sky was overcast throughout the build-up, with a moderate temperature and intermittent drizzle. The composition of the crowd evidenced a wide spread of ages and an even sex distribution, with a slight emphasis on younger female fans at the front of the queue. The mood of the crowd was good-natured with very little jostling and pushing observed and full cooperation in the search and ticket monitoring procedures was observed as the audience passed through the lane system.

The initial build-up at the entrances dispersed within as little as eight minutes subsequent to the opening of the gates. The flow rates were steady, supported by the minute-by-minute measurements recorded by the data collection team on Gate 9.

Immediately after passing through the gates, the audience was encouraged by the marshals using loud-hailers to slow down and to desist from running. There was a further natural barrier in the tree lanes that obscured the audience's view of the stage. Once past this natural barrier, the size of the site and the direct access to the front of stage made it impossible to prevent the audience from rushing to anywhere in the arena. The size of the arena and the lack of obstacles between the audience and the stage meant that any running at this point was not a hazard as groups of people running into the arena were sufficiently dissipated, causing no obstruction to others. Additionally, by the funnelling of the crowd towards the entrance points at either end of the secondary barrier, the final stage of access to the front of stage viewing area could be further controlled.

6.2.2 Day Two
The major difference in the conditions of the crowd gathering at the gates prior to the opening on day two was that the numbers that had arrived by 11:30am were far greater than on the previous day. The other notable difference between the two days was that there was uninterrupted sunshine and the

temperatures were far higher than those of the previous day. This difference in the weather is also reflected in the products brought to the event by the audience, identified in questionnaire one.

The access gates were opened to the audience at 11:40am, 40 minutes earlier than on the previous day. This change in time had not been communicated to the production crew working in the arena who were taken by surprise. There was still a forklift truck in the arena (although it had finished the clearance work which it had been engaged in) and another truck was driving towards an exit at the back of the arena as the crowd started to enter. The advantage of the barrier system was highlighted by this. Prompt action by the pit security team (who were also taken by surprise by the early opening time of the gates, but who reacted extremely well to it) were able to stop the crowd from gaining access to the front of the stage area until the forklift had exited into the backstage area. A similar incident occurred at the National Bowl on day two where Gate 6 opened before Gate 3 was ready, causing problems in the auditorium as those still working in the arena were taken by surprise.

The size of the crowd outside the gates at the time of the opening was reflected in the time it took for those working the gates and lanes to clear the initial build-up. This lasted approximately 40 minutes and the flow through the gates into the arena was calculated to be at approximately the same rate as that calculated on day one.

6.2.3 Day Three

The climatic conditions present on day three mirrored those on day two uninterrupted sunshine and high temperatures with a clear sky. The size of the crowd massed outside the gates prior to the scheduled midday opening time was also approximately equal to that on day two. The composition of the audience was similar to the other two days, showing a consistency in demographics. Due to the massing of the crowd at the entrances, it was again decided to open the gates earlier than on the first day. The gates were again opened 40 minutes earlier than the first day at 11:40, but in fact only 20 minutes earlier than the advertised time. The initial build-up took slightly longer to clear than on day two at around 45 minutes after the gates had opened.

6.3 The Measurement of Crowd Flow at Ingress: Cumulative Audience Totals

As outlined in the introduction, a modified research strategy for the measurement of the crowd flows at the ingress was adopted at the Robbie Williams shows, as this crowd flow measuring system was perceived to be more accurate and furnished the researchers with a more appropriate data set, which could be readily applied to the project. The institution of the new technique enabled the flow of people through the gates to be measured on an hourly basis. Such a system proved useful as the cumulative total of spectators in the arena at any point in the day could be ascertained from the results. The principle practical application of this research was to determine how many people remained at ingress gates and how many reverted to exit gates at any point during the day. Such information is crucial to ascertain immediate spectator totals and to assess management strategies at any point during the proceedings. Sufficient evacuation facilities can therefore be maintained in the event of an emergency. The modification in the technique is identified in the following passage:

- Focus of the research was now on one gate instead of all the gates. (The objective was to find a gate that would be in use throughout the day and where a reasonable number of lanes would be kept open).
- Data was collected on an hourly basis.
- A careful monitoring of the total number of gates in use at the time the flow data was collected was important. This was achieved by sending a team around the perimeter of the site at the same hourly interval that the flow readings of the lanes were being gathered. This could also be ascertained in future through radio contact.
- The use of a spreadsheet to calculate the hourly flow rate into the arena and the cumulative total at each hour.

Day One

Notes to table on facing page:
1. Gate 9 was used on Day 1
2. Each counter was responsible for the same two lanes, so the reading for Lane 1 is a combined reading for Lanes 1 and 2.
3. The average numbers coming in through the lanes every hour is

TIME	L1	L2	L3	L4	L5	L6	L7	L8	GATE TOTAL	TOTAL LANES	AV. PER LANE PER HOUR	LANES IN USE	HOUR TOTAL	CUMULATIVE TOTAL
Gates open										55		44		
12.20	401		795		558		529		2283	55	830	42	36,528	36,528
13.20	180		178		180		76		614	55	447	42	18,755	55,283
14.20	106		104		158		81	244	693	55	504	25	21,168	76,451
15.20	91		245		176		181		693	55	504	21	12,600	89,051
16.20	86		116		143		244		589	55	428	13	8,996	98,047
17.20	230		106		120		104		560	55	407	25	5,295	103,341
18.20	97		149		56		111		413	55	300	22	7,509	110,850

The Measurement of Crowd Flow at Ingress: Cumulative Audience Totals - Day One determined by working out the average hourly figure for every lane counted, then multiplying by the lanes in use for that hour. Data figures are for 30 minutes initially and then for 15 minutes after 13.20, meaning that multiples of 2 and 4 are applied to the gate totals.

4. Time given at the start of the count.

On day one, as the system was being utilised and the measurements for each hour were recorded, it was noticeable that the cumulative total was lower than would normally be expected. By 18:20, with the main support band Moby already on stage, it became apparent that a further 15,000 ticket-holders had still to access the venue. At first, this was assumed to be a problem with the spreadsheet or the data inputting, therefore the formulae were checked and re-checked. The same rigorous checks were also applied to the data. By this stage of the concert, the lane counters had been stood down and there was no further data being collected; in the same way, no record was being kept of the number of lanes that were still in use.

At the same time the data and formulae were being checked in the command and control centre, conflicting reports were being received concerning the traffic situation on the main roads leading to the Knebworth site. The police reports were not highlighting any unusual build-ups, but phone calls from people stuck on the northbound carriageways of the A1(M) were reporting that traffic was at a complete standstill and tailing back to south of Exit 6.

At this point, it was decided that a visual count should be maintained on Gates 6-9 which were the main point of entry for the audience that were still arriving. This was decided as these gates were closest to the main car-parking facilities and, by this stage, the people that were still arriving were doing so almost exclusively by car. The premise was, that providing a continual flow of people was still being recorded entering the gates, it could be assumed that the figures were reasonably reliable. If the flow was reduced for any prolonged period of time to a mere trickle (as would be expected for this stage at a concert of this size) then it may have signified a fundamental flaw in the counting system. In fact, the flow continued even longer than was either expected or usual at this type of event. At 9.30pm when Robbie Williams had been onstage for an hour, there was still a solid flow of people walking from the car parking areas, up the hill to the gates. Reactions from these people were all very similar, they had been stuck in traffic jams and congestion for times ranging up to two hours. One of the research organisers left the site at approximately 9.55pm, exiting by car through the backstage access route. As the road into Knebworth village crossed over the A1(M) he reported observing a long queue of traffic stuck on the northbound carriageway.

On Saturday August 2nd, the press and the radio reports widely reported the "traffic chaos" surrounding the event, highlighting one of the more polemic aspects of the organisation of the shows. This report deals with the traffic problem elsewhere, in the observations made on command and control and the role of the police at this event.

From the system employed to measure crowd flow ingress to the event, an immediate benefit for the crowd manager was identified. The devising of a system that calculated average flow rates through the lanes of the main gates, and by simultaneously monitoring the number of lanes in use for ingress, an approximate hourly total of spectators coming in to the venue could be ascertained. Through the aggregating of these hourly totals, the determination of a cumulative figure for the total number of people in the auditorium at any given time throughout the day could be ascertained. From the traffic problems experienced at the Robbie Williams concert, the system had inadvertently shown the merits for its usage in identifying accurate figures of those within the arena.

The other application of the cumulative count system is that it highlights the timing of the turning of lanes and gates that were initially utilised for ingress into exit lanes, or egress gates. However, in the example quoted in this study, the fact that the flow of people gaining access from the car parking areas to Gates 6 and 9 was constant right up to and during the first part of Robbie Williams' performance. This meant that the organisers had no choice but to keep open to staff the ingress lanes on Gate 6. Further queues at an entrance gate for the necessary search and ticket collection would have strained the tolerance of customers after the delays experienced with the traffic. This potential problem was averted by the security staff.

It must be pointed out at this juncture that from participant observation and interview the main reason ascertained for the steady flow of consumers to the Knebworth event was the billing of the show. The majority of the audience polled were not interested in the other artists on the bill and thus they arrived later as they were only interested in the main act. However, at the Eminem show the bill was sufficiently strong to attract the majority of the crowd to the venue before the show began and thus it can be ascertained that the bill for the event is an important element in the planning and execution of event strategies.

Day Two

TIME	L1	L2	L3	L4	L5	L6	GATE TOTAL	TOTAL LANES	AV. PER LANE PER HOUR	LANES IN USE	HOUR TOTAL	CUMULATIVE TOTAL
Gates open												
11.40								44		44		
12.40	557	1662	640	675	776	650	4960	44	827	42	27,639	27,639
13.40	949	140	554	1321	664	141	3769	44	628	42	26,383	54,022
14.40	449	662	560	433	419	504	3027	44	505	25	21,189	75,211
15.40	598	386	496	418	392	12	2302	44	384	21	9,592	84,803
16.40	814	573	747	1021	0	0	3155	44	789	13	16,564	101,367
17.40	218	449	445	363	0	0	1475	44	369	25	4,794	106,161
18.40	157	351	467	727	0	0	1702	44	426	22	10,638	116,798

The Measurement of Crowd Flow at Ingress: Cumulative Audience Totals - Day One - Day Two

Notes to table on facing page:

1. Gate 6 was monitored rather than Gate 9, since it was the preferred Gate for customers arriving on foot from the Car Parking areas, as it was the closer of the Gates.

2. This combined with the fact that there were fewer lanes used for ingress meant that the flow of people through Gate 6 was more constant.

3. The responsibility for the counting passed to the stewards working Gate 6, who clicked cumulative totals for the whole hour. The students monitored the number of gates open. It was hoped that this would lead to greater accuracy by providing a more accurate observation of the lanes in use at any given time.

The major difference between the first and second days of the concert was the volume of attendees arriving at the site prior to the scheduled gate opening time of 12:00 noon. The combination of this factor with a generally younger and more excitable audience, led to the decision to open the gates earlier than anticipated. Such a decision caused communication problems in the arena itself as not all of the production staff had been alerted that the gates were to be opened. The other factor which differed on day two was the weather, which had changed from the overcast and chilly air of the previous day to being sunny, cloudless and extremely warm. Another observation made as a result of the change in weather and a larger crowd massing outside the gates was the build-up of crowds at the site before gates opened did not translate to greater numbers being able to gain access into the auditorium during the first hour. Although there was an initial rush of those anxious to get to the front of the stage, this rush was not sustained. It was observed that people were content to spread themselves over the site as a whole and to enjoy the space that the site outside the perimeter fence offered. It was also observed that the concession stands outside the perimeter fence were doing excellent business throughout the day. The other facility that was in constant use, as expected, was the toilets.

Due to the alleviation of many of the traffic problems on the day, the flow of people into the auditorium was much more regular than on the previous day, with fewer lulls, giving rise to a steady growth in the cumulative figure for the day.

The organisers had warned the research team in advance that more tickets had been sold to coach companies on day 2, and therefore the crowd would arrive on site in much greater numbers from the coach parks, which were sited on the opposite side of the venue from the car parks. This was supported by both observation and video evidence which identified that by 14:30 there were large queues at Gate 2 which was the principle gate utilised by people arriving from the coach parks. At first it was assumed that this was a queue for the toilet facilities, which were located in that area. Closer observation indicated that the queue was in fact for the Gate. The reason for the large queue at this point was that there were still only 2 lanes open out of a possible 10 at Gate 2 and therefore the flow into the venue was extremely limited. It was observed that the security staff identified the problem and then remedied the situation by opening the remainder of the lanes and addressing the queue with a loud-hailer in order to instruct the attendees to move to the newly opened lanes. The queue was dissipated quickly and efficiently. It was perceived that the reason why this had occurred was that the security staff on gate 2 had assumed that the ingress pattern for the Saturday would be the same as for the Friday, when in fact the additional coaches had meant that far more people were going to use this gate to gain access to the auditorium. Thus, communication of the behaviour not only of the crowd and also transport patterns is vital for crowd strategies.

Whilst observing the crowd movement through the gates and into the arena it was identified that there was a significantly greater crowd density at around 18:30 in the arena on day 2 as opposed to day 1 at the same time. This was inevitable given the fact that the crowd on Friday had experienced delays in accessing the site, but it also meant that the conditions inside the arena became crowded and much more difficult to manage at a much earlier stage.

Day Three

Notes to table on facing page:

1. The method of data collection was exactly the same as for Day Two

The weather conditions on day 3 were similar to those on day two with the temperatures being slightly higher on the third day. In fact, the temperatures measured on this day made it one of the hottest days of the year. The crowd had again arrived on site earlier than on the first day and thus the gates were opened some twenty minutes before the scheduled time in order to alleviate the pressures caused by the build-up at the gates.

The fill-rates for the front barrier were approximately the same as on day two, indicating that this section of the audience had arrived early with the

TIME	L1	L2	L3	L4	L5	L6	GATE TOTAL	TOTAL LANES	AVERAGE PER LANE	LANES IN USE	HOUR TOTAL	CUMULATIVE TOTAL
Gates open												
11.40								44		44		
12.45	897	756	1200	1040	881	0	4774	44	955	32	29,357	29,357
13.45	692	564	765	774	541	0	3336	44	667	36	21,350	50,707
14.45	737	559	510	882	0	0	2688	44	672	30	24,192	74,899
15.45	664	116	793	875	0	0	2448	44	612	27	18,360	93,259
16.45	944	921	899	0	0	0	2764	44	691	19	18,657	111,916
17.45	743	689	952	0	0	0	2384	44	596	19	11,324	123,240

The Measurement of Crowd Flow at Ingress: Cumulative Audience Totals - Day Three

intention of claiming their place as close to the stage as possible. This was also evidenced from interviews and video evidence taken on the three days of the concert.

Similarly, as evidenced on day two, once the early rush had dissipated, a constant flow was observed throughout the rest of the day. Fewer dips in the numbers coming through the gates were observed, and consequently the filling of the arena at an earlier time than on days one and two was experienced. By 18:00 the flow had reduced considerably, rather than the more gradual tailing off that had been observed on day two and the continual flow on day one. The counts were double checked and the data collection scrutinised for possible errors. However, the observation of the arena and video evidence, led to the conclusion that the public had arrived on site earlier and had moved into the arena at the earliest opportunity. While the change in the weather from the Friday to the Saturday may have come as a surprise, people were more prepared for the sunny conditions on the Sunday and therefore more ready to enjoy a full day out. This is evidenced through the questionnaires where more sun block and caps were taken into the arena than on any other day.

6.4 Crowd Behaviour and Perceptions at the Eminem and Robbie Williams Events

6.4.1 Introduction

At the two events, 1800 questionnaires were completed at three different stages of the event. The first was taken prior to the event whilst the audience were queuing to gain access. The second was administered once the audience had entered the area and the third whilst the show was taking place. The following sections identify the responses of the attendees for each stage of the questionnaire process. The responses are then analysed and conclusions drawn.

The audience composition at the Eminem and Robbie Williams concerts differed in many ways and such differences are linked to the nature of the event and the genre of the artist. The audience for the Eminem event were mainly young, white and male, whilst the composition of those attending the Robbie Williams show were more family orientated, multi-cultural, and contained a wide range of ages and a more even distribution of male and female attendees. From the analysis of the events, it is clear that the differing composition of the two audiences had a marked effect on their behaviour.

6.4.2 Crowd Behaviour and Perceptions Before Entering the Event Arena

6.4.2.1 Findings

On soliciting responses from attendees outside the concert venue in relation to where they were going to observe the concert, the responses at National Bowl and Knebworth were very different. At the Eminem concert, 91% of attendees on the first day, and 60% and 86% of respondents on the following days identified the front of the arena as their preferred area for viewing the show. The rest of the responses for this event were evenly split between other viewing areas. However, at the Knebworth event, only 26%, 21% and 32% respectively for the 3 concerts were heading to the front to observe the event. The bar and merchandising areas featured heavily in other responses from Knebworth attendees.

It can be identified from audience responses prior to their entering the arena, that attendees are not aware of the configuration of the amenities and the event production inside the arena, so they can only guess from what they have seen on television or from experience of other concerts at the same or other arenas. Those arriving on the first day of each three-day event have even less of a reference point as they have seen neither broadcasts on the news of the event nor could they have been informed by others who have attended on previous days.

When ascertaining where respondents were heading once they had entered the arena, the responses differed from those given in answer to the first question. 86%, 53% and 74% of respondents at the Eminem show were heading to the front of stage area (a similar proportion to those identified in question 1), whereas at Knebworth only 41%, 43% and 46%, respectively, were heading to the front of stage area to view the show. A high percentage (21%, 27% and 16%) were going to look for somewhere to sit down and others were going to make their way to the bar, the rim, or the centre of the arena.

The organisation of the queuing at the Eminem concert was perceived to be poor by 62% of the attendees on the first day. 47% thought it was poor on day two with 42% finding the queuing to be well marshalled. On day three, 48% found it good and 36% poor. At Knebworth on the first day, 90% found the queuing system to be good, with the initiative, resourcefulness and pro-activity of the attendees with regard to clothing and other items essential to the enjoyment of the day being particularly important.

At Eminem on all three days, water was the most frequently sourced addition to take into the event. However, on day 2, less than 50% of people carried water with them. Sun block was also thought to be important but still only 45%, 27% and 12% carried this commodity although the days were extremely hot and sunny (although days two and three were less so than day one). Coats and caps were also worn or taken into the National Bowl. However, at the height of the good weather only one-third of all people were wearing or possessed caps and coats. At Knebworth, the water situation was very similar to that of the Bowl where 39%, 48% and 53% of attendees brought or carried water into the event. On the first day, 100% of those interviewed had coats but this was then reduced to 26% and 10% respectively on the following days of the event. Concomitant to this was the rise in caps of 28%, 43% and 63% respectively. The trend was similar with sun block where 9%, 48% and 66% of people took in sun block over the three days as the heat of summer intensified. Although only 1% of the Eminem attendees took rugs into the venue, 12%, 12% and 29% of the Knebworth attendees utilised rugs at the Robbie Williams event over the three days.

The majority of National Bowl attendees took protective action or protective items into the bowl through guesswork, common sense or by chance, but about a quarter of the attendees drew on experience. At Knebworth over a third of people attending used past experience to identify their concert requirements, whilst the other two-thirds relied on common sense or guesswork.

6.4.2.2 Analysis

The foregoing findings determined the following:

The differing audience profiles, the genre of music, and both macro and micro environmental factors were in many ways responsible for the choices made by both Eminem and Robbie Williams attendees before the two events. The information available, past experience and serendipity play a large part in the way in which the audience perceive the event in advance of it taking place. Although previous experience of concerts does help to prepare attendees for the event, the very nature, size and scope of an event is often remembered in such a way that only the good parts spring to mind. Heat, rain, coldness in the evenings, thirst and other identifiable problems are often overlooked in an attempt to ensure that concert preparations identify the least possible encumbrance to the attendee. An example of this is that on a hot day many attendees take water and sun block, but do not carry coats. Where an event is hot during the day, due to lack of cloud cover, they can be extremely cold at night and thus problems can be caused for those without sufficient or appropriate clothing.

The main preoccupation of the Eminem audience when identifying where they were going to watch the show from was to make straight to the front to be near to the performer on stage. From participant observation and interview, this area was identified as the best place to watch the concert. Therefore, anyone dealing with the management and safety of the event must be aware that such behaviour is likely, and at such events, the majority of the crowd may at some stage try to reach the barrier in the arena. This evidence is supported by video footage of the crowd entering the arena, fill-capacities and participant observation. In the case of the Knebworth attendees, a wider range of viewing points were chosen, including the bar, the merchandising/food service areas and seated areas/areas where a rug could be put down. Such areas were cited as just as important as heading to the front of the arena to watch the show. The wider range of choices when watching the Robbie Williams concert alleviated the pressure at the front of stage area which reduced the possibilities of an accident at this pressure point, although (as will be identified later in this section), caused hazards elsewhere in the event. It can therefore be surmised that on entry to the arena, the majority of Eminem attendees perceived that they were heading straight to the front of the arena by the barrier, whereas just under half of the Knebworth attendees were heading toward this area. However it is also clear that although about 25% of the Knebworth attendees identified the front of stage area as where they would go to on first entering the arena, 33% wished to watch the artist as close to the front as possible. The rim, the centre, and anywhere where a seat could be identified or created were important drivers in the Knebworth attendees' event orientation.

The organisation of the queuing at National Bowl was not perceived by the audience to be adequate, although their perception of this did improve over the three days of the event. At Knebworth, the queuing mechanisms on the first day were perceived as extremely good but the confidence in the queuing mechanism was reduced over the following two days of the event.

This was mainly due to the following: Initially two entrances were utilised to gain access to the National Bowl (Gates 3 and 6), but from participant observation and video footage, it was clear that the restrictions at Gate 3 impeded access to the arena. A constriction took place on the narrow access road and bridge leading up to the entrance (Gate 3) slowing entry into the arena causing a bottleneck and thus congestion. At Gate 6, the wider access and funnelling made entry to the concert arena more effective and efficient. The security personnel and managers recognised the problems on the first day, but it was impossible for them to act upon their intelligence (due to the volume of attendees queuing early to enter the arena) until the second day, when a more organised and streamlined queuing system could be put into operation. On the third day, further changes and improvements were made identifying good practice and observation and this is reflected in the responses from attendees, participant observation and video footage.

The queuing system at Knebworth identifies the obverse of the scenario at the National Bowl, where the attendees indicated progressive dissatisfaction with the queuing mechanisms as the days of the concert proceeded. From participant observation and video footage, it is clear that on the first day, due to the traffic problems, the slow flow of attendees facilitated an adequate queuing system. However, due to the traffic problems caused on the A1 and surrounding roads, those organising the queuing mechanisms could not foresee possible problems when the traffic restrictions were addressed and as such, changes could not be made until the third day. The news broadcasts regarding traffic problems sent out the message that concert goers should set off earlier to be sure of reaching the venue in time for the show, and thus differing crowd behaviour and dynamics ensured that the queuing mechanisms were inadequate on days two and three of the event. This example identifies the difficulties for the security/stewarding, organisers and managers in identifying changes in trends and behaviours that may force quick changes in crowd management strategies.

The foregoing analysis suggests that the audience composition at the two events is directly related to the queuing patterns. At the Eminem concert the majority of the audience queued for over three hours to ensure that they had the best possible chance of viewing the concert from an advantageous position near to the front of the arena. At Knebworth, however, the queuing time was generally reduced to less than thirty minutes. The family composition of the audience was more concerned with enjoying the day out and the event than finding a place near to the front, thus a steadier flow of attendees was observed at Knebworth when compared with the National Bowl. As the capacity of the National Bowl was 65,000 for the Eminem event and the capacity of Knebworth 125,000, an increased number of gates were in operation at the Knebworth event (as stipulated in the licence) to ensure a greater volume of attendees was able to access the arena in a short time scale, alleviating the pressure outside the gates. On days two and three of the National Bowl concert, further entrances were utilised to alleviate the pressure at Gates 3 and 6 and thus good practice was identified where a problem on one day was rectified on subsequent days. It was also clear from audience responses at Knebworth that the show bill was such that the majority of the audience were only interested in one act and this factor was one of a number of factors responsible for the steady entry of attendees over a six-hour period. Whereas the bill at the Eminem concert was such that the total audience was inside the venue in just over two hours.

It is apparent from the forgoing analysis that the directions and information given in advance of the concerts were thought to be better for the Knebworth venue than Milton Keynes. From participant observation and interviews with attendees, it was perceived that although there was a good communication system servicing the National Bowl, the information given was too general and was not sufficient for concert-goers.

The analysis suggests that a large majority of concert-goers recognise that water is an essential commodity to take to concerts and it is also clear that the initial weather at the home base influences the products taken into the concert arena. At the Eminem concerts, sun block was perceived to be more important on day 1 than on the other two days. This is in line with the initial weather on the day and conditions the preceding day, which influenced whether sun block was taken into the arena. Only one third of the audience, however, had either caps or coats and failed to realise that when the day was hot and had no cloud cover the nights would be concomitantly cold. At Knebworth, the audience was more perceptive of the concert environment. 100% of the audience carried coats on the first day, but as the weather became hotter, this was reduced drastically down to 10% by the third day. However, there was a concomitant rise in the use of caps or hats from 28% to 68% by the third day, showing that the weather forecast has a distinct bearing on the audience behaviour. There was a similar rise in sun block from 6% on day one to 60% by day three. In interviews the rise in sun block and caps was in response to newspaper, radio and television reports about the concert. A much larger number of people utilised rugs at the Knebworth event than the Bowl event, evidencing the number of families and the differing priorities of the two types of crowd.

The research identifies a more streetwise audience visiting the Knebworth event than the National Bowl show, as a greater number of people identified what they would need for the concert from experience. From participant observation, video footage and interviews, it was clear that a large number of Eminem attendees were visiting their first large concert event, whereas at Knebworth the audience was visiting the event during the course of a normal summer event programme.

6.4.3 Crowd Perceptions and Behaviour When First Entering the Arena

6.4.3.1 Findings

Many of the attendees stated that before entering the arena they would be making their way to certain areas; the actuality of this was tested. A higher percentage of Eminem attendees headed for the front of stage area (47%, 51% and 42% respectively on the three days) from those attending Robbie Williams (35%, 24% and 39% respectively on the three days). The bar was another popular alternative with between 10% and 20% of attendees at both concerts heading towards the bar on first entering the arena over the three days. The attendees at Knebworth were twice as likely to look for somewhere to sit than those at National Bowl. These findings identify differing perceptions between the behaviour of the audience outside and inside the arena.

The attendees at both events perceived that they were relatively safe at the front of the arena by the barrier (77%, 93% and 94% respectively at Eminem and 97%, 83% and 62% respectively at Robbie Williams). However, from interviews and video footage it is clear that the crowd is less safe and more vulnerable in the areas behind the mosh pit.

The majority of Eminem attendees, when asked where they would be watching the main act from once they were in the arena, identified that they were going to try to get as close to the front as possible (67%, 79% and 44% respectively on the three days). The Robbie Williams attendees, however, were less specific and although between 40% and 50% of them were making for the front of the arena each day, there was a wide spread of other areas towards which attendees were headed towards to observe the concert. These included the delay tower, in front of the big screens, the centre of the arena, the bar and the rim.

When asked which support product services were important at an event and which were not, sun block was thought to be the most important, where on all but one of the six days positive responses to this product totalled over 25% and on the last day of the Knebworth show reached 42%. Waterproof sheets and capes were extremely popular on the first day of the Robbie Williams show with 34% and 24% respectively. In the case of hats and caps, there was a reduction in the perception that these should be provided over the three days from 15% to 6% at the Eminem show. However, the opposite was identified at Knebworth with a concomitant increase from 8% to 25%.

When asked whether respondents perceived that they had brought the right clothes for the event, the majority of people responded positively to this question (79%, 76% and 91% at National Bowl and 86%, 81% and 95% respectively at Knebworth). However, on the first day of the Eminem event 20% of the audience perceived that they had not brought the right clothes and on the second day of each concert 23% and 19%, respectively, thought that they were ill prepared for the weather.

6.4.3.2 Analysis

From the foregoing findings, a number of issues can be identified.

It is clear from the first questionnaire that the majority of Eminem fans perceived that they will head to the front of the stage when entering the arena. However, the actual numbers who do head to the front of stage area on entering the arena is approximately 50% less than those who originally perceived this as a goal on entry. From participant observation, video analysis and interviews, two major reasons are responsible for this reduction. The first is that only a certain percentage of the attendees are able to secure a place at the front and this becomes evident when the attendees enter the arena. Video footage shows that attendees, when running into the arena stop and weigh up their options and then decide whether it will be advantageous to them to head for the front. The second reason is that once the attendees enter the arena and notice the layout, they make other decisions from those first experienced. This is highly visible from interviews and from video footage. A similar picture is shown from the Robbie Williams data where fewer attendees actually make their way to the front of the barrier than was first expected from the initial responses ascertained. From video footage, participant observation and interview data it is clear that, due to the lack of knowledge of the actual scale and impact of the event set up, customer perceptions outside the event change very quickly on entry. It is also clear that although people perceive that they will be able to concentrate their efforts on heading to the front, the marketing of the bar and merchandising areas, as well as alternative places to sit and watch, all impinge on crowd behaviour.

The perception of safety at the barrier by attendees at both concerts is high as they are aware of the stewarding presence and thus feel more assured of their safety. The institution of a barrier and stewards to control the barrier, as well as visible first aid services, give a high perception of safety. However, further back from the barrier, the picture is very different; attendees feel vulnerable and this was especially evident just behind the 'mosh pit' area at both concerts. At Eminem the majority of injuries at the event were caused by bottle throwing incidents. These had their greatest impact behind the mosh area and in the centre of the arena. Attendees did not perceive a safety presence in this area, nor did they perceive that if an accident happened, help would be available quickly and efficiently. On interview, attendees identified security watchtowers or some kind of zoning system to make the central concert areas safer. At Knebworth, the two major areas of unsafe practice were identified as directly behind the mosh pit and at the periphery of the arena where the audience could see neither the stage nor a screen. As a large percentage of the audience in the area behind the mosh pit were sitting down, when the main artist came on stage the sudden rush of the audience caused pushing, crushing and instability. Had the artist been of a different genre with a more volatile fan base, more serious incidents may have occurred. In the area directly behind the mosh pit, it is very difficult for the security personnel to intervene if an incident occurs. One such incident occurred at Knebworth where the positioning of the toilet block with all the doors facing one way meant that it could take up to an hour to move around the block to utilise the entrances. Therefore, customers climbed over the toilets to access them, causing a security incident, as it was perceived that they were climbing over the gates and fences. A circular toilet block would have alleviated the situation.

A large number of attendees at the Knebworth event could not see a stage or a screen. These attendees became extremely agitated and disgruntled with the management of the event. Many tried to push their way from the back and the sides of the arena into the main body of the audience, but this caused further problems due to the density of the crowd. Many people sitting down and taking up more than their allotted 0.5 m² caused the increase in density. At the front of the event at both concerts, there were often more than four people within a 0.5m² area. Such inconsistencies need to be addressed.

The identification of a vantage point from where to watch the main band is also modified once inside the arena. Outside the arena the majority of Eminem attendees wanted to watch the artist from as near to the front as possible.

However, once inside this perception changed and a wider range of vantage points from which to watch the concert are utilised. It is clear that the behaviour of attendees changes as options become available and thus it would be difficult to plan a crowd strategy from the information gathered prior to an event. Thus the greater the control exerted by the managers of an event, the less likely it is that risks and hazards will occur. A specific and controllable system is needed from the outset.

The key services required at the event varied depending on the weather conditions. For example, on the hottest days it was perceived that sun block was key and also, when there was a chance of rain, coats, plastic sheeting and ponchos were perceived as vital. When sunny, caps or hats were thought to be essential. However, it is clear from the foregoing analysis that attendees require all of these services whatever the weather, as through either negligence or ignorance many concert attendees are unprepared both physically and psychologically for concert attendance. Such services should also be cheap and readily available as they are essential to the event. At this point, the price of merchandising and non-consumables must be raised. It is a sellers' market at concert events as they can charge a high premium on such items, since they have as it were a 'captive audience'. However, attendees are aware that they are being overcharged for such items and this does cause a certain amount of consternation and angst, which affects crowd behaviour. From those interviewed it is clear that many attendees refused to buy the merchandise as it had become prohibitive due to the high costs. The analysis also suggests that the overall amount of merchandise sold for one-off events would increase if the prices were lowered, as more attendees would be able to afford the lower priced merchandising and those willing to spend a set amount of money on merchandising would buy more than one item.

Many attendees and those stewarding the event identified the need for welfare services at concerts. From the foregoing analysis it can be identified that there are a wide range of attendees who fail to recognise the different elements required at a concert and the difference between a large concert event and an event on the television observed in their own home environment. Due to this problem, many attendees encounter serious issues both physically and psychologically where they do not have the constitution that equips them to function in such an environment and the use of welfare services is crucial to enable them to cope. To deliver an event without such services is opening up the debate of duty of care and the possibility of lawsuits being brought against promoters for not recognising the needs of the audience. From participant observation and interview, so many attendees at the Eminem concert arrived for the first time at such an event and were totally unprepared for anything which might have happened.

Those attending concerts are often under the misapprehension that they have brought the right clothes and product to enjoy the day safely. However, many attendees perceive a T-shirt as weatherproof and an umbrella as a sunshade and beer as a thirst quenching drink. Little guidance is given to concert attendees on such matters except at festivals such as Glastonbury, where there is a safe concert guide. Orange also compiles a concert pack to assist attendees in surviving the weekend. A low-cost concert pack with a sachet of sun block, a plastic poncho, a small bottle of water and a safety sheet would go a long way to alleviating many of the problems associated with concert safety.

6.4.4 Crowd Perceptions and Behaviour at the Barrier

6.4.4.1 Findings

The majority of attendees identified the perception of the barrier area at the Eminem concert as vital, fun and exciting over the three days of the concert. Only 27%, 24% and 29%, respectively, perceived that there are negative connotations to the institution and usage of a barrier. However, this still constitutes over one quarter of those interviewed at the concert. At Knebworth, a high percentage of the attendees perceived the barrier as fun, vital and exciting with 15%, 7% and 28% identifying the barrier area with negative connotations, which is on average less than the attendees at the Eminem concert.

The importance of being at the front at the concert is identified as vital by between 94% and 97% of the attendees at the Eminem concert, and between 87% and 95% of the Robbie Williams attendees agreed with this statement.

The idea of instigating regulations to stop crowd surfing were met with some anger and rebellion by Eminem attendees; 29%, 6% and 20% showed anger at such an idea, whilst 36%, 4% and 13% identified rebellion. 12%, 24% and 57%, respectively, showed understanding or welcomed regulations on moshing. At Knebworth 83%, 81% and 84% showed an understanding of why regulations were needed and welcomed such regulations to make the pit a safer place.

Where measures were identified to enhance the enjoyment of the crowd at concerts the Eminem attendees unanimously recognised special security measures and specialist pit training as essential to the development of a safer pit environment. Similarly, attendees at the Robbie Williams concert identified special security measures and pit training as key elements in the development of safer pit areas. At the National Bowl, the introduction of CCTV, segregation of the pit from other areas, and padded floors and barriers were also perceived to be key factors in the development of health and safety at concerts. At the Knebworth concert, specific first aid, CCTV, padding and the introduction of compulsory water fountains also featured heavily in the identification of developmental measures to enhance the safety and well-being of the audience.

From those attending the Eminem concerts, an average of 87% did not support regulations that prohibited moshing and crowd surfing, whereas between 32% and 60% of those attending the Robbie Williams concerts supported regulations which prohibited moshing and stage diving.

6.4.4.2 Analysis

It is apparent from the foregoing findings that a large number of concert attendees view the barrier as an area of danger even though many of them frequent the barrier area on a regular basis. However, those at the Knebworth event perceive less danger at the barrier. From video footage, interviews and participant observation, the barrier area at the Eminem event was a far more dangerous place to be than that at the Robbie Williams event. However, it is only more dangerous because of the activities taking place there and not because the dangers of crushing and trampling were not in evidence at both events. From participant observation and video footage supported by interviews, the management of the front of barrier area was perceived as good and that the majority of incidents were dealt with effectively and efficiently. The gang fighting in the pit on the second day of the National Bowl event was well organised and specifically targeted and thus impossible to eradicate, as staff members are not equipped to deal with such incidents.

It is clear from the foregoing research that being at the front of the concert is vital to the enjoyment of the event for a large number of attendees at an event, and that those further back in the crowd perceive that they are somewhat disadvantaged by their placement. Many of the attendees at the Robbie Williams concert were not able to see the stage or a screen and thus felt cheated by their experience of the event. On interview, one attendee identified that there should be a price differential on the tickets for those in certain areas of the arena where either the stage was obscured or where they did not have access to a screen or both.

The audience at the National Bowl event replied negatively to questions regarding the development of safety measures at the barrier. The stopping of moshing and stage diving were not well received by this audience. However, a high percentage of those attending the Robbie Williams event welcomed more safety measures to enhance their enjoyment of the event. Both Eminem and Robbie Williams attendees identified specialist pit training and further security measures as the way forward to curbing problems in the pit area. It is noticeable that the audience mainly preferred the introduction of further training and security measures in the pit area rather than the stopping of moshing and diving altogether, as it was perceived that this action would make the pit area a more dangerous place owing to the constricting of activity and the behaviour associated with such banning. CCTV, padding on floors and barriers, water fountains at the front of the stage and specialist first aid were all thought to be elements that would improve the safety in the pit area. It is again clear that the audience does not want moshing and stage diving stopped but wants them to be made safer by the concert promoters. Segregation was also mentioned as a measure where different areas of the arena are segregated to enable a safer environment.

The majority of Eminem fans were against the banning of crowd surfing whereas 60% of those at Robbie Williams supported safer measures in the development of the mosh area. Again, the foregoing research points towards the composition of the audience at the two events influencing how safe or dangerous the event becomes. Thus, the genre of music and the artist are key features determining the behaviour of the audience. In the previous question, many attendees felt that the artist should be more responsible in the way in which they motivated the audience and that they could diffuse many situations before they got out of hand, although from experience it is difficult to facilitate such responsible action.

6.4.5 Conclusions from this Section of the Research

- The composition of the audience, which is dictated by the genre of music, and the audience demographic has a significant effect on the behaviour at an event affects crowd dynamics and strategies.
- Behaviour is influenced by both internal and external macro and micro environmental factors, such as the weather and viewing restrictions.
- Problems on one day of an event can affect event strategies and

thus careful consideration and monitoring of the event can initiate the implementation of modifications to existing strategies on future days or events.

- Customer perceptions of an event change from exposure to external and internal environmental factors, which influence crowd strategies.
- The alleviation of both physical and perceptual barriers to an event can enhance the enjoyment of the audience.

Therefore, the genre of music and the artist are key features determining the behaviour of the audience. In the previous question, many attendees felt that the artist should be more responsible in the way in which they motivated the audience and that they could diffuse many situations before they got out of hand, although from experience it is difficult to facilitate such responsible action.

6.4.6 Conclusions from this Section of the Research

- The composition of the audience and thus crowd dynamics and strategies.
- Behaviour is influenced by both internal and external macro and micro environmental factors, such as the weather and viewing restrictions.
- Problems on one day of an event can affect event strategies and thus careful consideration and monitoring of the event can initiate the implementation of modifications to existing strategies on future days or events.
- Customer perceptions of an event change from exposure to external and internal environmental factors, which influence crowd strategies.
- The alleviation of both physical and perceptual barriers to an event can enhance the enjoyment of the audience.
- Work on price differentials at events so that those wishing to access certain areas pay more than others do.
- A zoning system to make security and crowd monitoring easy to develop 89% and 67% found the events well marshalled on subsequent days, which is dictated by the genre of music, and the audience demographic has a significant effect on the behaviour at an event

There was a differing perception of queuing times and access to the venue at the two events. At Eminem on day 1, 69% of attendees queued for over three hours, on day 2, 31% with a further large majority queuing for over 1-2 hours before the gates opened, and on day 3, 67% queued for over 3 hours. At Knebworth, the majority of the crowd queued for less than 30 minutes. 64% on day 1, 81% on day two, and 44% on day 3. On day three, however, over 85% queued for less than three hours.

The information (how to get there, conditions, what to take, etc.) released prior to the Eminem event was thought to be average by those at the Eminem concert (Day 1, 43% good/very good 36% poor/very poor. Day 2, 38% good/very good, 42% poor/very poor and Day 3, 55% good/very good, 40% poor/very poor) whilst at Knebworth 65%, 75% and 67% of the attendees respectively found the information to be good or very good.

7 A CRITIQUE OF ESTABLISHING CROWD CAPACITY AND DENSITY AT AN OUTDOOR CONCERT EVENT ATTRACTING A MASS CROWD
(Produced by Mick Upton)

7.1 Crowd Safety at Mass Crowd Concerts

An announcement by the Rolling Stones in 2003 that they intended to play to a crowd of half a million people that summer in Canada brought a great deal of criticism from the crowdsafe website with regard to crowd safety planning. Following the concert, however, one newspaper quoted a Toronto Police spokesperson as follows: *"Slick, safe and smooth. That's how the security operation went for 450,000 people"* (Toronto Star 2003).

During the same summer, Robbie Williams played to a total of 375,000 people in a series of three concerts at Knebworth Park, Hertfordshire, England. Criticisms of these concerts were also published on the web; this time it was ticket buyers that expressed concern for their personal safety. Some of these critics put forward the view that concerts that attract a mass crowd had now reached a level where they were simply too big to be managed safely. A subsequent concert debrief however appears to indicate that accident/injury rate recorded at all three concerts was extremely low. It appeared that the critics of mass crowd concert events had over-reacted.

While a great deal of credit must be given to all those involved in the organisation of the aforementioned events, it may also, however, be a serious mistake to simply dismiss criticism of the events. It is still important that if only a very small number of ticket buyers express concern over their personal safety that their fears are investigated. It is possible that the rise in popularity of a mass crowd concept will perhaps bring with it hidden risks that some promoters are not fully aware of. In order to widen the crowd safety debate further this paper critiques a current method for establishing crowd capacity and density at a green field site and then warns of the powerful pressure loads that can be generated by a crowd mass. A 'mass crowd' is defined in this paper as 100,000+

persons in a given arena. The paper concludes by offering suggestions for improving green field site arena design. These suggestions do not claim to give a definitive answer to all problems associated with crowd management and strategy but rather they create a starting point for further discussion.

7.2 Current Practice

Guidance to aid the concert organiser has been available in the UK since 1974. Current guidance is published in the UK under the title 'The Event Safety Guide', known as The Purple Guide, as mentioned earlier. The Purple Guide advises that crowd capacity and density for a green field site can be measured based on two people per square metre ($0.5m^2$) with a clear view of the stage. The guide stipulates that the final figure reached is dependent on the availability of sufficient exit capability. This calculation is commonly applied in an international context to the establishment of crowd capacity at outdoor concert events. The notion that this simple calculation can automatically resolve capacity and density problems is, however, fundamentally flawed, as it does not take into consideration how people interpret space as a concept.

At a pop concert of long duration, people are likely to want to sit down, particularly in warm weather. When they do so they occupy at least twice the space that was planned for them. People trying to get to facilities or purchase food or drink will find it extremely difficult to move over people who are sitting or even lying on the ground and medical and security teams needing to get into the crowd have the same problem. New arrivals not finding space might assume that the arena is full or even overcrowded, when in fact conditions comply with agreed levels stated within current guidance. When everyone stands to see the headline act on stage, people on the fringe of the crowd might rush to take advantage of newly available space. In circumstances where this happens, conditions are ideal for triggering a dynamic or lateral crowd surge.

Sight lines are obviously an important factor at a major outdoor concert event. To ensure maximum safety standards, however, it is necessary to review conditions that might affect the horizontal line of view to the point of focus (stage or screen). Ground conditions should be the start point for this review. Slopes will naturally cause crowds to move forward. Alternatively, flat ground that does not drain off after an earlier rainfall will encourage people to seek dryer conditions. These situations can both be considered as potential causes of localised high density. These factors will also influence the positioning of crowd control barrier systems. A barrier that is positioned on a slope or on poor ground is unlikely to be effective and has in fact inherent dangers associated with its positioning.

The question of exit calculation is a source of debate among researchers. Practitioners utilising the recommended guidance based on theoretical concepts of space and measurement argue that such guidance simply does not apply in practical conditions. Such theory argues that flow has an optimum density. If this density is surpassed the obtainable rate decreases (Stanton & Wanlas 1991). When considering a mass crowd exit and its relationship with capacity, it would appear that more research is needed. As, if current exit calculation methods subsequently prove to be wrong, a disaster could result, particularly in an emergency evacuation when the arena needs to be cleared very quickly.

7.3 Pressure Loads

In a 1992 seminar paper, American planner John Fruin, pointed out that virtually all crowd-related incident deaths are caused by *compressive asphyxia*, not as a result of being trampled on by a panicking crowd, as often reported by the news media. There is no fixed point at which death occurs from being subjected to an intolerable pressure load. A British Home Office (1973) report cited two fatal cases:

a) Death of one male is estimated to have taken place when subjected to an estimated load of 1400 lbs (over six kn) in fifteen seconds.
b) A man died when subjected to an estimated load of 260 lbs (1.1 kn.) for 4.5 minutes.

Later experiments reported by Hopkins, Pountney, Heyes and Sheppard (1993) concluded that males and females were able to withstand pressure loads in the region of 140lbs - 180 lbs. (approximately 800 Newtons) when they were able to push against a fixed barrier to gain breathing space. Current medical opinion is that in conditions where the human body is subjected to a higher static pressure load of approximately 300lbs (1.1 kn) on the chest cavity beyond 2.5-3 minutes, the brain begins to starve of oxygen and permanent injury may be caused. Beyond 3 minutes death may occur at any time.

An intolerable pressure load can be caused in a number of ways at a concert, for example:

- High crowd density or a lateral or dynamic surge that converts to a static load. In these circumstances, it is common for those persons right in front of the barrier to push backwards off the barrier in order to gain space to breathe. This can then subject people further back from the barrier to a two-way horizontal load as people at the back press forward.

- A crowd collapse can occur as a result of a dynamic or lateral surge, individuals fainting, ground conditions or cultural behaviour. If a crowd collapse occurs, an intolerable vertical load is imposed on the victim(s) at the bottom of a pile of bodies very quickly. A crowd collapse can occur *anywhere* within a crowd mass.

When due consideration is given to the above, it would appear that a risk assessment based on a $0.5m^2$ calculation and current exit theory is far too simplistic a concept on which to establish capacity and density.

7.4 Arena Design

Over two thousand years ago, the Romans demonstrated that it was possible to design for crowd safety. By creating self-contained sections within the Coliseum, Roman planners maximised pedestrian flow during ingress and egress and controlled density for a crowd of 60/80,000 people (estimates of capacity for the venue vary). Crowd migration was catered for by a system of inter-communicating passages, gangways and stairs. The Roman quadrant design concept remains the basis for stadium design.

It is suggested in this paper that green field site arenas could introduce a zone approach to safety design. Each zone could be colour coded or numbered. Independent ingress and egress points would serve each zone and controls established within the system to prevent unwanted crowd migration. Advanced publicity could advise ticket buyers of their position in the arena. For each zone to operate as an independent viewing area, it is essential that facilities (toilets, water, emergency points, welfare etc.) and vendor points (bars, merchandise and catering) be placed within it.

By designing emergency lanes and emergency access gates in the system, medical teams could move more easily to all parts of the crowd, enabling them to triage a patient virtually at the scene and evacuate serious injuries far more easily. The emergency lanes would also assist security teams to enter a crowd to deal with disorder or to extract persons in distress. Careful calculation could ensure that emergency lanes and gates are capable of evacuation from one zone to another if necessary. The appendix to this paper provides a simple illustration of a possible zone system. As stated previously, the illustration provided is only intended as a starting point for further discussion. It is freely acknowledged that arena design is subjected to many variables.

With regard to establishing safe zone occupancy and density levels, each zone would have to be calculated individually and the sum total of all zones presented within a risk assessment as the proposed capacity level. In terms of calculation method, this paper supports the view of Sime (1993) who argued that insufficient attention to the way that people behave in a crowd and the relationship between behaviour and systems design, are major factors in crowd disasters. The calculation would therefore need to be based on psychology (the way that people think and act) X engineering (systems design).

7.5 Conclusions

This paper has provided only a few examples to support an argument that current practice for the establishment of capacity and density levels at a mass concert event is a high-risk strategy. Changing a system that has been in common use at temporary venues for decades will, however, be difficult. It will require a complete rethink of our approach to the often complex issues of risk analysis and risk assessment. It will also require a long hard look at the issue of responsibility.

It is common practice today for the site manager to design the arena to include such elements as location of facilities and vendors and barrier system types. Headline acts might also stipulate a particular barrier system should be in place, and tour security staff might inspect the installed system. The crowd manager, who might be from a private security company, then comes in, possibly only to suggest design of ingress and egress systems. On the day, however, the crowd manager is expected to take responsibility for crowd safety overall. In such circumstances, it is often the case that the manager will either have to accept possible high-risk conditions or incur the cancellation of the show. Current practice is therefore illogical as three or four people have had input into system design.

If the issue of responsibility is to be addressed it requires one person to accept total responsibility for all aspects of crowd safety. This includes all pedestrian flow calculations, calculations for localised zone evacuation, queue systems, barrier systems that comply with current European directives for manual handling, and contingency plans for emergency evacuation - all of which should be clearly documented in the form of a risk assessment. It is accepted here that my conclusions cannot be implemented immediately. It is also possible that other people might come forward with better ideas; therefore crowd safety is an issue that requires a great deal of further discussion and research before it is possible for the industry to demonstrate a visible safety cultures.

Appendix:

For discussion purposes, illustrated below is a possible design for a pop concert with an attendance of 100,000 persons at a green-field site.

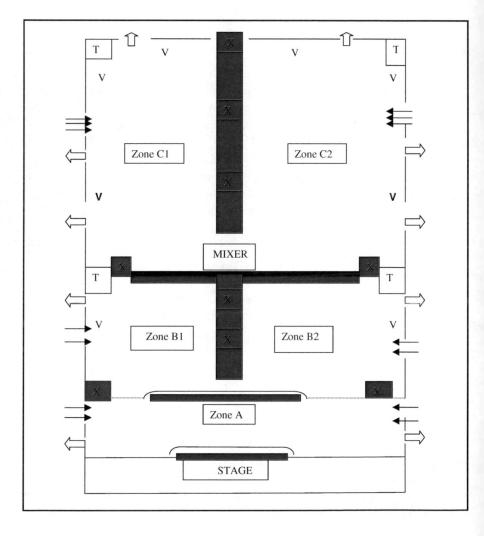

Key to Diagram:

⇨	= Exits
⟶	= Ingress: ingress gates would convert to exits as a zone nears capacity
T	= Toilet blocks
V	= Vendor points
▮	= Emergency lane ▮ = emergency exit gates

8 CONCLUSIONS TO THE REPORT

Taking into consideration all aspects of the foregoing analysis, it is clear that there are three major elements concerned with the development of crowd management strategies. These comprise the physical nature of the venue chosen for the event, the composition and behaviour of the crowd, and the management experience and strategies employed by those overseeing and promoting the event. The identification of the venue for an event is both complex and fraught with problems. Both macro and micro environmental factors affect each decision a promoter or manager makes when choosing a venue. Size, situation, site, geographical location, communications, licensing services and many other factors are taken into account when the final decision on the venue is made. The choosing of the venue site, however, is separate from the other two major elements of management strategy and audience composition, although the three are linked through the interface between these elements in the concert event itself.

The behaviour of the audience is influenced by many and varied macro and micro environmental factors. The foregoing analysis suggests that consumer intelligence is of paramount importance in the delivery of a safe concert environment. However, such consumer intelligence is often not fed into a developing strategy until the post mortem of an event. In reality, consumer intelligence should be constantly utilised to update and to create the underpinning body of knowledge through which a concert strategy is modified during the time frame of the event. The strategies employed by concert promoters and security companies alike are key elements in the delivery of a safe concert environment and thus these strategies need careful and considered appraisal, not just to feed into the planning stages or at the post mortem, but to keep the strategy a live entity throughout the concert process.

The body of knowledge intrinsic to a safe concert environment is divided into three complementary but mutually exclusive areas. Firstly, the information disseminated to the prospective attendees and thus the pre-event intelligence available to the concert manager prior to the event, is useful in setting the scene for the event. Management information pertains to the crowd composition, previous events by the artist or at the venue, weather reports, traffic reports and communication systems, as well as how prepared the audience might be for the event itself. From the consumer perspective, these elements are also important, but more important is a clear idea of what to expect on reaching the venue, what the consumer will need for the day and information on welfare, first aid, and what commodities will be available on site. The more relevant the information disseminated to the consumer, the more effective and efficient the crowd strategies will be if such intelligence is identified prior to the event and fed into modifications to a strategy.

Secondly, arrival at and entry to the event is an important factor to take into consideration. From the arrival of the audience at the event, the length of time the audience has been queuing, audience demographics, how the audience arrived, and the behaviour of the audience outside the gates, can give the concert planners a great deal of information on what to expect during the event. However, what the audience perceives to be the concert environment from outside the event changes as they gain entry, thus giving the consumer as much information prior to the show as possible enables the managers to meet the expectations of the crowd and thus alleviate many of the problems associated with the event. From the audience perspective, they are there to enjoy themselves and thus they will perceive any inconvenience as incompetence on behalf of the management staff. By reducing such problems, the behaviour of the crowd can be manipulated. However, from the analysis it is also clear that welfare services are of vital import to the smooth running of the event. The non-regular concert attendee is not aware of the inherent dangers of sunstroke, the size of the arena, difficulties in mobilisation, how cold it becomes in the evening, and the problems caused by the arrival of rain or darkness. To alleviate problems, which start even before the gates open, a welfare team on site is crucial. Trained personnel in this area are important to deal with may of the problems, which the everyday member of security or staff of the venue are not trained to deal with. The utilisation of a welfare team can stop small problems getting out of control and take the pressure from the crowd managers.

Thirdly, once inside the arena the majority of the audience head towards the front of the auditorium if it is at all possible and thus this area fills up first. After this area has reached capacity, different audience groupings choose specific locations in which to congregate to watch the show. Research into the fill-capacities identify that ease of access to an arena facilitates a faster filling rate and fewer problems with crowd congestion at access and egress points.

Taking each of the three areas related to the concert environment and identifying how crowd intelligence can be beneficial to already existing strategies, it is clear that a main benefit to those managing the event is the reduction of the pressures on personnel involved with such events. The elements identified in the foregoing analysis inherent in the crowd intelligence can be utilised in a rolling risk assessment, enabling the modification of strategies throughout the event. Such modification enables crowd managers to keep in step with the changing audience environment and thus reduces pressure on those working at the event. Thus, the management of the crowd in such a fluid environment as the concert event enables full dialogue and idea exchange enhancing the safety aspects over the time-frame of the event. Such fluid strategies were in evidence at both the National Bowl and Knebworth; however, there was also evidence of slow response rates to periodic issues where strategies were inflexible until it was too late. The idea of living documentation is important to ensure that risks and hazards are cut to a minimum.

Fill-capacity is reliant on clear access to the pens and barriers. Where barriers to access are identified, the fill-capacity in the restricted area is reached in a longer period than that of the unrestricted area. To avoid a disproportionate pressure build-up at the front of the stage it is important that restrictions to those wishing to gain access to this area be minimised as far as possible, facilitating equal fill at both sides of the stage. Such equality would alleviate unequal pressure build-up. Alternatively, stricter stewarding of the access to the front of the stage (where a set number of attendees are allowed entry from both stage right and stage left) would regulate the pen build-up more efficiently. Utilising facilitators in the pen area at the start of the event would enable uniformity in crowd density and model build-up at the front of the stage, enhancing safety and creating an efficient and effective front-of-stage strategy.

It is identified in the foregoing analysis that pressure build-up outside the National Bowl was far greater than that at the Knebworth site, where crowd congestion was more easily dispersed. Such ease of dispersion was mainly due to the greater number of lanes and gates in operation on entry to the arena and the lack of constriction at the gates to the Knebworth site. The accessible wide-open spaces on entry to the arenas at both venues caused confusion and elicited a large number of attendees to run and fall as a result. There is an obvious lack of control once attendees have entered the arena and this can not only cause injuries from over exuberance and the speed of entry, but also uneven build-up in many areas. If the arena were to be segregated, far greater control of the audience would be attained. The problems of injury and risk are increased by changing gate times without fully informing those working in the arena, thus the need for a universal communication system is quite clearly identified in such a case. Changing the times must enable due warning to be given to those working. Allied to the pressure build-up both outside and inside an arena, cumulative totals are important in identifying the number of attendees inside the venue at any one time. Correct identification of the numbers inside the venue and the number still to arrive at an event enables the correct proportion of ingress and egress gates to be maintained in operation throughout. Guesswork in such a crucial area could cause untold problems if litigation was invoked and the proportion of ingress to egress gates was found to be incorrect for the numbers in the event. Strategic, tactical and operational levels can all be informed by cumulative totals, fill-capacities and crowd behaviour intelligence systems.

The identified guidance figure of $0.5m^2$ per person is not robust enough to stand up to scrutiny at most events where crowd migration, spread, dispersal and density vary from act to act and hour by hour. The institution of smaller, controlled zoned areas would enable greater control over an audience and make the monitoring of a smaller number of people much easier. Occupation of more space per person and good sightlines are two elements that enhance crowd enjoyment. Pressure loads at mass crowd gatherings can be well above safe levels. Crowd collapses are most likely to occur at events where there are long periods between artists, and sudden crowd rushes occur as an artist comes onstage. Such rushes by the crowd and constant pressure on barriers can cause compressive asphyxia as the pressure at the front of the barrier causes push back and the pressure from behind continues unabated with added pressure from crowd rush as the main artist comes on. Thus this area of crowd control urgently needs to be reviewed.

An observation from the Report suggests that a fully integrated event control room within which a combined emergency liaison and crowd management team could operate would be beneficial in the concert environment. The police, fire, ambulance, security services and local authorities could inhibit duplication of roles and responsibilities through such a measure and increase effective and efficient management of the event. However, such developments would need further study before the legitimacy of such a centre could be identified. The audience perceive the events researched as relatively safe. This is related to good management techniques and strategies, as well as the work carried out by the event planners and managers on site during the event. However, a disaster may only be seconds away at any point during an event and this research has shown that careful but flexible planning and strategies coupled with a fluid risk assessment carried out periodically during each day of each event, would minimise risk as long as the risk assessment is a central core of management and strategy. It is clear that the smaller the audience the greater amount of control can be exerted and the easier intelligence is to gather, as small audiences are more likely to be controlled through micro rather than macro strategies. The greater the audience and more uneven the site and the distribution of the crowd, the more imponderables arise and the more pinch points are possible.

This paper has described and analysed a number of pertinent areas for further discussion and analysis and provides a foundation for further studies into crowd behaviour and management.

REFERENCES

HSE (2001) **The Event Safety Guide 2001.** (b): *Incident Control Room (the co-ordinating group and location)*: Chapter 4 *Major Incident Planning*, page 35 paragraph 212

HSE (2001) **The Event Safety Guide 2001.** *Venue Capacity/Occupant Capacity*: Chapter 2 Venue and site design, page 15 paragraph 87 and Chapter 3, *Fire Safety*, page 22 paragraph 122

London HMSO **Exit Capacity.** Chapter 5, page 44 paragraph 5.22

Fruin J.J. (2) 1993 **Engineering For Crowd Safety**, ed. Smith R.A. & Dickie: The Causes and Prevention of Crowd Disasters: *Prevention of Crowd Disasters by Crowd Management, P104.* Elsevier Science Publishers B.V.

London HMSO **Guide to Fire Precautions in Places of Entertainment and Like Premises** (a) 1990: *Occupant Load Factors*: Chapter 5, page 43 paragraph 5.20

London HMSO **Guide to Fire Precautions in Places of Entertainment and Like Premises** (b) 1990

London Stationary Office **Guide to Safety at Sports Grounds 1997**: *Recommended rates of passage*: Chapter 9 *Circulation – Egress and Emergency Evacuation*, page 80 paragraph 9.6

Home Office (British) 1973: **Crush Barriers Strengths and Spacings**: Home Office Advice Note issued March 1973.

Hopkins et al 1993: **Crowd Pressure Monitoring**: Published Seminar Paper in 'Engineering for Crowd Safety', ed. Smith R.A. Dickie J.F.: Elsevier Science Publishers B.V.

Sime J.D. 1993: **Crowd Psychology and Engineering: Designing for People or Ballbarings**: Paper presented to 'Engineering for Crowd Safety'; International Conference, Institution of Civil Engineers, London, 17th-18th March 1993. Jonathan Sime Associates, 26 Croft Road, Godalming, Surrey GU7 1BY.

Smith 1991: Quoted by Stanton R.J.C. & Wanless G.K. in Published

Seminar Paper, *Pedestrian Movement* in **Engineering For Crowd Safety**; ed. Smith R.A. & Dickie J.F.: Elsevier Science Publishers B.V. 1993.

Stanton & Wanlas 1991: **Study of Railway Termini**: Published Seminar Paper in 'Engineering for Crowd Safety', ed. Smith R.A. Dickie J.F.: Elsevier Science Publishers B.V.

Toronto Star 2003: National newspaper Review of a Rolling Stones concert in Toronto, Canada, published 31.7.2003.

ENTERTAINMENT TECHNOLOGY PRESS

FREE SUBSCRIPTION SERVICE

Keeping Up To Date with

A COMPARATIVE STUDY OF CROWD BEHAVIOUR AT TWO MAJOR MUSIC EVENTS

Entertainment Technology titles are continually up-dated, and all major changes and additions are listed in date order in the relevant dedicated area of the publisher's website. Simply go to the front page of www.etnow.com and click on the BOOKS button. From there you can locate the title and be connected through to the latest information and services related to the publication.

The author of the title welcomes comments and suggestions about the book and can be contacted by email at: chris.kemp@bcuc.ac.uk

Titles Published by Entertainment Technology Press

ABC of Theatre Jargon *Francis Reid* **£9.95** ISBN 1904031099
This glossary of theatrical terminology explains the common words and phrases that are used in normal conversation between actors, directors, designers, technicians and managers.

Aluminium Structures in the Entertainment Industry *Peter Hind* **£24.95**
ISBN 1904031064
Aluminium Structures in the Entertainment Industry aims to educate the reader in all aspects of the design and safe usage of temporary and permanent aluminium structures specific to the entertainment industry – such as roof structures, PA towers, temporary staging, etc.

AutoCAD – A Handbook for Theatre Users *David Ripley* **£24.95** ISBN 1904031315
From 'Setting Up' to 'Drawing in Three Dimensions' via 'Drawings Within Drawings', this compact and fully illustrated guide to AutoCAD covers everything from the basics to full colour rendering and remote plotting.

Basics - A Beginner's Guide to Stage Lighting *Peter Coleman* **£9.95** ISBN 190403120X
This title does what it says: it introduces newcomers to the world of stage lighting. It will not teach the reader the art of lighting design, but will teach beginners much about the 'nuts and bolts' of stage lighting.

Basics - A Beginner's Guide to Stage Sound *Peter Coleman* **£9.95** ISBN 1904031277
This title does what it says: it introduces newcomers to the world of stage sound. It will not teach the reader the art of sound design, but will teach beginners much about the 'nuts and bolts' of stage lighting.

A Comparative Study of Crowd Behaviour at Two Major Music Events
ISBN 1904031250
Chris Kemp, Iain Hill, Mick Upton **£7.95** ISBN 1904031099
A compilation of the findings of reports made at two major live music concerts, and in particular crowd behaviour, which is followed from ingress to egress.

Electrical Safety for Live Events *Marco van Beek* **£16.95** ISBN 1904031285
This title covers electrical safety regulations and good pracitise pertinent to the entertainment industries and includes some basic electrical theory as well as clarifying the "do's and don't's" of working with electricity.

The Exeter Theatre Fire *David Anderson* **£24.95** ISBN 1904031137
This title is a fascinating insight into the events that led up to the disaster at the Theatre Royal, Exeter, on the night of September 5th 1887. The book details what went wrong, and the lessons that were learned from the event.

Focus on Lighting Technology *Richard Cadena* **£17.95** ISBN 1904031145
This concise work unravels the mechanics behind modern performance lighting and appeals to designers and technicians alike. Packed with clear, easy-to-read diagrams, the book provides excellent explanations behind the technology of performance lighting.

Health and Safety Aspects in the Live Music Industry *Chris Kemp, Iain Hill* **£30.00**
ISBN 1904031226
This title includes chapters on various safety aspects of live event production and is written by specialists in their particular areas of expertise.

Health and Safety Management in the Live Music and Events Industry *Chris Hannam*
£25.95 ISBN 1904031307
This title covers the health and safety regulations and their application regarding all aspects of staging live entertainment events, and is an invaluable manual for production managers and event organisers.

Hearing the Light *Francis Reid* **£24.95** ISBN 1904031188
This highly enjoyable memoir delves deeply into the theatricality of the industry. The author's almost fanatical interest in opera, his formative period as lighting designer at Glyndebourne and his experiences as a theatre administrator, writer and teacher make for a broad and unique background.

An Introduction to Rigging in the Entertainment Industry *Chris Higgs* **£24.95**
ISBN 1904031129
This book is a practical guide to rigging techniques and practices and also thoroughly covers safety issues and discusses the implications of working within recommended guidelines and regulations.

Let There be Light - Entertainment Lighting Software Pioneers in Interview
Robert Bell **£32.00** ISBN 1904031242
Robert Bell interviews an assortment of software engineers working on entertainment lighting products.

Lighting for Roméo and Juliette *John Offord* **£26.95** ISBN 1904031161
John Offord describes the making of the production from the lighting designer's viewpoint - taking the story through from the point where director Jürgen Flimm made his decision not to use scenery or sets and simply employ the expertise of Patrick Woodroffe.

Lighting Systems for TV Studios *Nick Mobsby* **£35.00** ISBN 1904031005
Lighting Systems for TV Studios is the first book written specifically on the subject and is set to become the 'standard' resource work for the sector as it covers all elements of system design – rigging, ventilation, electrical as well as the more obvious controls, dimmers and luminaires.

Lighting Techniques for Theatre-in-the-Round *Jackie Staines* **£24.95** ISBN 1904031013
Lighting Techniques for Theatre-in-the-Round is a unique reference source for those working on lighting design for theatre-in-the-round for the first time. It is the first title to be published specifically on the subject, it also provides some anecdotes and ideas for more challenging shows, and attempts to blow away some of the myths surrounding lighting in this format.

Lighting the Stage *Francis Reid* **£14.95** ISBN 1904031080
Lighting the Stage discusses the human relationships involved in lighting design – both between people, and between these people and technology. The book is written from a highly personal viewpoint and its 'thinking aloud' approach is one that Francis Reid has used in his writings over the past 30 years.

Model National Standard Conditions *ABTT/DSA/LGLA* **£20.00** ISBN 1904031110
These *Model National Standard Conditions* covers operational matters and complement *The Technical Standards for Places of Entertainment*, which describes the physical requirements for building and maintaining entertainment premises.

Pages From Stages *Anthony Field* **£17.95** ISBN 1904031269
Anthony Field explores the changing style of theatres including interior design, exterior design, ticket and seat prices, and levels of service, while questioning whether the theatre still exists as a place of entertainment for regular theatre-goers.

Practical Guide to Health and Safety in the Entertainment Industry
Marco van Beek **£14.95** ISBN 1904031048
This book is designed to provide a practical approach to Health and Safety within the Live Entertainment and Event industry. It gives industry-pertinent examples, and seeks to break down the myths surrounding Health and Safety.

Production Management *Joe Aveline* **£17.95** ISBN 1904031102
Joe Aveline's book is an in-depth guide to the role of the Production Manager, and includes real-life practical examples and 'Aveline's Fables' – anecdotes of his experiences with real messages behind them.

Rigging for Entertainment: Regulations and Practice *Chris Higgs* **£19.95**
ISBN 1904031218
Continuing where he left off with his highly successful *An Introduction to Rigging in the Entertainment Industry*, Chris Higgs' new book covers the regulations and use of equipment in greater detail.

Rock Solid Ethernet *Wayne Howell* **£24.95** ISBN 1904031293
Although aimed specifically at specifiers, installers and users of entertainment industry systems, this book will give the reader a thorough grounding in all aspects of computer networks, whatever industry they may work in. The inclusion of historical and technical 'sidebars' in this book makes for an enjoyable as well as informative read.

Sixty Years of Light Work *Fred Bentham* **£26.95** ISBN 1904031072
This title is an autobiography of one of the great names behind the development of modern stage lighting equipment and techniques.

Sound for the Stage *Patrick Finelli* **£24.95** ISBN 1904031153
Patrick Finelli's thorough manual covering all aspects of live and recorded sound for performance is a complete training course for anyone interested in working in the field of stage sound, and is a must for any student of sound.

Stage Lighting Lighting Design in Britain: The Emergence of the Lighting Designer, 1881-1950 *Nigel Morgan* **£24.95** ISBN 190403134X
This book sets out to ascertain the main course of events and the controlling factors that determined the emergence of the theatre lighting designer in Britain, starting with the introduction of incandescent electric light to the stage, and ending at the time of the first public lighting design credits around 1950.

Stage Lighting for Theatre Designers *Nigel Morgan* **£17.95** ISBN 1904031196
An updated second edition of this popular book for students of theatre design outlining all the techniques of stage lighting design.

Technical Marketing Techniques *David Brooks, Andy Collier, Steve Norman* **£24.95**
ISBN 190403103X
Technical Marketing is a novel concept, recently defined and elaborated by the authors of this book, with business-to-business companies competing in fast developing technical product sectors.

Technical Standards for Places of Entertainment *ABTT/DSA* **£30.00** ISBN 1904031056
Technical Standards for Places of Entertainment details the necessary physical standards required for entertainment venues.

Theatre Engineering and Stage Machinery *Toshiro Ogawa* **£30.00** ISBN 1904031021
Theatre Engineering and Stage Machinery is a unique reference work covering every aspect of theatrical machinery and stage technology in global terms.

Theatre Lighting in the Age of Gas *Terence Rees* **£24.95** ISBN 190403117X
Entertainment Technology Press is delighted to be republishing this valuable historic work previously produced by the Society for Theatre Research in 1978. *Theatre Lighting in the Age of Gas* investigates the technological and artistic achievements of theatre lighting engineers from the 1700s to the late Victorian period.

Walt Disney Concert Hall *Patricia MacKay & Richard Pilbrow* **£28.95** ISBN 1904031234
Spanning the 16-year history of the design and construction of the Walt Disney Concert Hall, this book provides a fresh and detailed, behind the scenes story of the design and technology from a variety of viewpoints. This is the first book to reveal the "process" of the design of a concert hall.

Yesterday's Lights – A Revolution Reported *Francis Reid* **£26.95** ISBN 1904031323
Set to help new generations to be aware of where the art and science of theatre lighting is coming from – and stimulate a nostalgia trip for those who lived through the period, Francis Reid's latest book has over 350 pages dedicated to the task, covering the 'revolution' from the fifties through to the present day. Although this is a highly personal account of the development of lighting design and technology and he admits that there are 'gaps', you'd be hard put to find anything of significance missing.

Go to www.etbooks.co.uk for full details of above titles and secure online ordering facilities.